The Magistracy
at the Crossroads

The Magistracy at the Crossroads
Edited by David Faulkner with the assistance of Sally Dickinson
Foreword Lord Dholakia

Published 2012 by
Waterside Press Ltd
Sherfield Gables
Sherfield on Loddon
Hook, Hampshire
United Kingdom RG27 0JG

Telephone +44(0)1256 882250
E-mail enquiries@watersidepress.co.uk
Online catalogue WatersidePress.co.uk

ISBN 978-1-904380-86-3 (Paperback)   **ISBN** 978-1-908162-13-7 (E-book)

Cover design © 2012 Waterside Press. Design by www.gibgob.com

UK distributor Gardners Books, 1 Whittle Drive, Eastbourne, East Sussex, BN23 6QH. Tel: +44 (0)1323 521777; sales@gardners.com; www.gardners.com

North American distributor International Specialized Book Services (ISBS), 920 NE 58th Ave, Suite 300, Portland, Oregon, 97213-3786, USA. Tel: 1 800 944 6190 Fax 1 503 280 8832; orders@isbs.com; www.isbs.com

Cataloguing-In-Publication Data A catalogue record for this book can be obtained from the British Library.

Printed by CPI Group (UK) Ltd, Croydon, CR0 4YY.

e-book *The Magistracy at the Crossroads* is available as an ebook and also to subscribers of Myilibrary and Dawsonera (for ISBN see above).

The Magistracy at the Crossroads

Edited by David Faulkner

With the assistance of Sally Dickinson

Foreword by Lord Dholakia

WATERSIDE PRESS

CONTENTS

THE AUTHOR OF THE FOREWORD

Lord Dholakia's interest in criminal justice and penal affairs has seen him involved in the Sussex Police Authority, the Police Complaints Authority and he has been a council member of the Howard League for Penal Reform since 1992 as well as a member of the editorial board of the *Howard Journal of Criminology*. From 1992-1996 he also served as a member of the Ethnic Minority Advisory Committee of the Judicial Studies Board. He became a peer in 1997, was a frontbench spokesperson on Home Affairs after serving as an assistant whip between 1997 and 2002, and was elected to the post of Party President of the Liberal Democrats in 1999 and in 2002. In November 2004, he was elected joint Deputy Leader of the Liberal Democrat Peers. Lord Dholakia was a magistrate in West Sussex for 14 years.

FOREWORD

In 2011 we celebrated 650 years of the magistracy but we did this with an eye on a somewhat uncertain future. Despite government ministers from all parties making statements of support, magistrates have been undermined by court closures, considerable reductions in legal staff, the increased use of district judges (magistrates' courts) and a national administration that has removed local involvement in deciding priorities. In contrast, localism and the involvement of local communities and citizens have been promoted by successive governments—leaving magistrates to wonder how the two opposing trends could be reconciled.

So, in 2012 we are looking to the future development of the magistracy—and what we have already discovered is that there may be many potential ways forward.

I was pleased to be asked to chair the Magistrates' Association's public engagement programme which will help to provide a greater understanding of people's views on the future of summary justice and the role of magistrates. The report of that programme will inform future policy debate and development—and this series of essays complements that report.

This book brings together ideas from a wide range of well-informed contributors on the way forward for the magistracy. Which direction will it be? As professional judges; members of a mixed tribunal; community champions; problem-solving justices; professional jurors; members of review committees? The possibilities are as diverse as the roles that magistrates have already played in their long history—and perhaps they can all be part of the future of this remarkable body of people.

Lord Dholakia

April 2012

THE EDITORS

David Faulkner has been a Senior Research Associate at the University of Oxford Centre for Criminology since 1992. He was a Fellow of St John's College Oxford from 1992 until 1999 and served in the Home Office from 1959 until 1992, becoming Director of Operational Policy in the Prison Department in 1980 and Deputy Secretary in charge of the Criminal and Research and Statistics Departments in 1982. His latest book, *Where Next for Criminal Justice?,* written with Ros Burnett, was published in October, 2011.

Sally Dickinson is Policy Director at the Magistrates' Association and has worked for the association since 1992. She is currently leading on the Magistracy in the 21st Century Policy Development Programme. She studied theology at Bristol University and completed a law degree at Bristol Polytechnic (now the University of the West of England) whilst working in the civil service. She worked for the Law Society for several years before moving to London in 1985 to join Apex Trust, the ex-offender employment charity. Sally Dickinson is a parish councillor in Kent and a trustee of Fair Trials International.

Details of the individual contributors appear before their respective chapters.

Dedicated to the members of the Magistrates' Association
— past, present and future

INTRODUCTION

David Faulkner

Nature of the Magistrates' Role

Few institutions have as long and continuous a history as the magistracy in England and Wales. Throughout the 650 years of their existence, justices of the peace have provided a form of predominantly voluntary service with a duty to do justice both on behalf of the Crown by keeping the peace among the sovereign's subjects, and on behalf of the people themselves by maintaining the conditions necessary for a peaceful and civilised life. Their role could be seen as one the foundations for democracy and social and economic progress. Several of the writers who have contributed to this publication refer with justifiable pride to the magistracy's achievements and traditions.

Magistrates have over the years had a variety functions, including the provision or oversight of places of detention; organizing the earliest police forces in the form of watchmen, beadles and Bow Street Runners; reading the Riot Act; and being prepared to hear from police court missionaries who subsequently developed into probation officers. In later years magistrates came to play major roles as members of visiting committees in prisons, of watch committees, police authorities and probation committees.

Nowadays it is usual to think of the main function of magistrates as being to 'do justice' by sitting in court and conducting a trial, pronouncing judgement, sentencing offenders following their conviction (including after a plea of guilty), or making orders in relation to children. They do however have several other important functions such as granting search warrants and monitoring the requirements of drug rehabilitation orders.

Composition of the Magistracy

Magistrates were originally chosen because of their position in society. They were the community leaders of their time, enjoying social status and respect according to the standards of the period, although in a very different social context from that of the present day. They owed their authority and legitimacy not only to the status conferred by their appointment and the powers placed upon them by statute, important though they were, but also to their own qualities of leadership, integrity and respectability.

The composition of the magistracy has changed, especially in more recent years. Magistrates, at first usually men, came to be appointed from a wider range of social backgrounds and occupations such as nationalised industries, other public sector organizations and trade unions. Many of those bodies encouraged their workers to serve as magistrates and gave them reasonable time away from their work in order for them to do so. Later developments included the appointment of more women, so that there are now more or less equal numbers of men and women, and of members of minority groups who are now reasonably well-represented in proportion to their numbers in the population as a whole. Commercial and financial pressures and sometimes privatisation have however reduced the numbers who can afford to take time away from their work or give their employers the commitment they demand whilst also taking time out for training and to attend court, and efforts are still needed to widen the range of social, ethnic and cultural backgrounds from which magistrates are drawn. As Kate Green points out in *Chapter 9,* the lay magistracy remains a major national resource which is not always fully recognised, understood or exploited.

Efficiency and Professionalisation

Like every other public service, magistrates' courts have been under pressure from successive governments to be more efficient, cut costs and reduce delays. Governments and magistrates themselves have been concerned to improve the quality of the justice that magistrates' courts deliver,[1] and at the same time to safeguard their judicial independence. Courts and courthouses have been closed, and increasing numbers of paid and legally qualified district judges (formally stipendiary magistrates) have been appointed. There has been pressure from government, and from some magistrates themselves, to 'professionalise' the lay magistracy and to bring it more into line with the higher, legally qualified, professional judiciary through measures such as training, the introduction of mentoring and appraisal, and compulsory training in a range of competences (as they are known) and related skills.

None of the contributors to this collection argues for greater professionalisation in that sense, but Louis Blom-Cooper (*Chapter 2*), Audrey Damazer (*Chapter 3*), Heather Hallett (*Chapter 10*) and Howard Riddle (*Chapter 15*) favour a closer integration of the lay and legally qualified judiciary, for example through mixed panels in which lay members would be able to make their own distinctive contribution and which would be less reliant on the judicial expertise of their legal advisers. Howard Riddle also describes how magistrates have had to respond to an increasing volume of new legislation, sentencing guidelines and judicial guidance, all of which have affected the way in which they exercise their discretion on a daily basis and added to the demands made upon them. Audrey Damazer describes in *Chapter 3* how the social context has become increasingly complex, especially for the family courts.

Magistrates' judgements are also more closely scrutinised by the media. Successive reorganizations, management reforms and tighter financial controls have left magistrates with little control over the administrative functioning of their courts, and although their judicial discretion has been protected it has come to be exercised within an increasingly tight managerial framework. Courts cannot be exempt from the demands of efficiency and accountability which must apply to any public service, but magistrates also have to consider the implications of doing 'right to all manner of people … without fear or favour, affection or ill will' in situations involving strong public feeling, political pressure and limited resources.

Andrew Ashworth (*Chapter 1*) and Aubrey Fox (*Chapter 4*) stress the importance of procedural justice and effective communication, and Professor Ashworth expresses concern that a disproportionate emphasis on performance measured by criteria such as speed or cost could come to affect the quality of justice itself. Criteria such as those can provide important management information, but they do not define what justice is or what it is for.

Inhibitions and Discouragement

The expansion in the magistracy's membership has been accompanied by a progressive contraction in the roles and functions which it performs. Most of its wider functions such as those relating to prisons, police, probation and licensing have been abolished or reduced in their scope and significance. Magistrates have been inhibited from becoming engaged in activities outside the court setting, for example in cross-agency arrangements affecting the wider criminal justice system, or engaging with voluntary organizations which help offenders or support victims of crime. The inhibitions have not for the most part come from any formal, still less statutory, restriction or guidance. They stemmed in the first instance from a proper concern to safeguard the magistracy's independence and so its authority and legitimacy. In a climate where there is a greater readiness to challenge authority of all kinds, a pervasive awareness of risk and aversion to it, and increasing political sensitivity and greater readiness to challenge public institutions, there has been a natural concern that the institution or an individual magistrate might be thought compromised if the public sensed that there was too close an association with a particular organization, interest or point of view. The unspoken message from government, from Crown Court liaison judges, chairmen of benches, clerks to justices and other court legal advisers could understandably be, 'If in doubt, don't do it'.

The Magistracy under Pressure

For those and other reasons, magistrates have felt themselves to be under pressure for a number of years. They have sensed that their role and status have been threatened; that the principle of 'local justice' has been undermined; it has become harder for them to be seen, or to see themselves, as representing their local communities; and there is a view in some parts of the central bureaucracy—and possibly elsewhere—that lay magistrates may no longer be needed at all and that in a modern system of justice the work should be done entirely by qualified professionals. Magistrates may not be paid, so the argument goes, but the resources that are needed to support their selection and training and to pay their allowances are considerable when compared with district judges, quite over and above general running costs which can be measured by the day, hour and minute. On the other hand, a recent survey of members of the judiciary, court staff and professional and lay users of the magistrates' courts (Ministry of Justice, 2011) found that lay magistrates were thought to be more connected with their local communities, perhaps more fair and open-minded and more 'democratic' as compared with district judges. They might be more expensive, but the responses and the evidence were inconclusive on that point.

Frances Gibb refers to that sense of uncertainty in *Chapter 5,* but she points out that the magistracy is also becoming more effective in its relations with government and the media, and believes that no government is likely to seek to abolish the lay magistracy in the foreseeable future. But a danger may remain that its role, influence and significance could be gradually attenuated until the very idea of volunteer judges comes to be seen as a quaint historical relic, existing on the fringe of an ever more professional, managerialist and perhaps more commercially driven and mechanical system of justice.

Given the present economic pressures on all elements of society and public service, it would be unrealistic to expect any relaxation of the demands for efficiency and economy, or any reopening of courts which have been closed. It is hard to see how the interests of justice could be served if magistrates were routinely to try and carry out their judicial functions more locally in places such as schools, libraries, supermarkets or police stations, or in prisons (other than in exceptional cases involving high security). A more promising area for exploration may be the various forms of 'community' or 'neighbourhood' justice, where important developments are already taking place and where, regardless of the future of the lay magistracy, there is a strong and arguably compelling case for reform and for a coherent, consistent and principled approach. Barry Godfrey (*Chapter 7*), Roger Graef (*Chapter 8*), Heather Hallett (*Chapter 10*), Rod Morgan (*Chapter 12*) and Nicola Padfield (*Chapter13*) all in different ways refer approvingly to the possibilities which lie in that direction.

Expanding the Magistrates' Role—Community Justice

The expression 'community justice' is used in several ways. It is sometimes a general expression used to refer to sentences served in the community, as distinct from sentences of imprisonment, or to the work which statutory or voluntary criminal justice agencies do in the community. Or it may be associated with programmes such as community service, now called 'unpaid work' or 'community payback', where offenders do work which is of benefit to the community, often of a kind which has been proposed by the community itself.

Community justice can however be understood and applied in ways which are more positive and dynamic. It can be developed within the court setting, or outside the courts altogether. Within the court setting, there are now numerous examples, both from Great Britain and especially from the United States of America, of what are coming to be called 'problem-solving justice' or 'problem-solving courts' (or sometimes in the academic literature 'therapeutic jurisprudence'). Experiments in both countries reflect a desire to move the focus of the court system from a standardised, mechanistic concentration on processing cases to solving the local community's problems of crime and antisocial behaviour, and giving them a greater voice in the administration of justice.

Problem-solving courts in New York claim considerable success in reducing crime and improving rates of compliance with court orders. In England the North Liverpool Community Justice Centre, modelled on the Red Hook experiment in New York, was based on a combined magistrates' court and Crown Court centre, presided over by a single judge, with the intention that it should be closer and more in touch with its local community and its social concerns and that it would involve that community much more closely in the work of the court. In that way the 'community' would gain a sense of ownership and empowerment and efficiency would be improved. An evaluation by the Ministry of Justice (2007) showed improvements in efficiency, but not much impact from engagement with the community, and the need for a special building had made the centre an expensive undertaking. Similar courts seem unlikely to be established in the foreseeable future.

More promising developments may be two one-stop justice centres which house the courts, police, Crown Prosecution Service, victim and witness support, probation and youth offending services under a common roof, especially if they can expand the role which magistrates might be able to play. None of those forms of community justice include provision for magistrates to play the more active or distinctive role of which they should be capable, but there may now be more opportunities for them to do so.

Further examples in England include specialist domestic violence courts, drug courts and mental health courts. An especially valuable function for magistrates might be in requiring suitable offenders to return to court at appropriate intervals so that their progress can be reported to the court and their success can be recognised and if possible rewarded.

Outside the Court

If some of the discouragements from participating in outside affairs could be removed, the understandings concerning participants' roles improved and the less justifiable demarcations relaxed, magistrates would be enabled to play a larger part in the expanding forms of community justice which operate outside the court setting. Examples could be as members of bodies such as probation trusts, neighbourhood justice panels and police and crime panels; taking part in activities such as restorative justice; or working with any of the numerous voluntary organizations which are concerned with reducing crime and rehabilitating offenders. Another possibility favoured by Andrew Ashworth, Rod Morgan and Nicola Padfield would be for magistrates to exercise a form of oversight for the use of non-judicial penalties such as on-the-spot fines, not to review individual cases but to consider the extent and patterns of their use and to make comparisons between different areas and over different periods of time.

Such activities could be broadly of three kinds. One would be in providing help or support for people such as offenders, ex-offenders, victims of crime or those at risk of committing offences or of having offences committed against them, whether as an individual volunteer or as a trustee or manager of an organization, usually a charity, which organizes help and support. A second would be as a member of an authority or a board which has a statutory or contractual responsibility for providing a public service in an area such as prisons, probation or policing. A third would be in holding a position where the person has some formal role or authority over others, for example in restorative justice or neighbourhood resolution.

Three important questions arise. The first is the 'added value' which magistrates' involvement in such activities would bring to the organization or the activity concerned, or to the magistracy itself. The second concerns the principles, rules, protocols, understandings and mechanisms according to which their involvement would be encouraged, permitted or restricted, and the means and authority for doing so. The third, to which Aubrey Fox refers in *Chapter 4*, relates to the nature of magistrates' accountability, and whether new functions would require a form of accountability to the public which goes beyond their accountability to the higher courts and the Lord Chancellor.

In the first type of activity it could be expected that the magistrate would perform his or her role in the same way as anyone else, and the fact of being a magistrate would only be incidental. A person's position as a magistrate would not as such bring any special value to the organization or activity, but the background of their judicial skills and training might well do so, for example in encouraging fair and balanced decision-making in the organization as a whole. Their involvement might also have value to the magistracy by enabling them to bring their knowledge, experience and understanding to the bench—in its judgments in particular cases, in considering its approach to particular types of cases, and perhaps in giving it more credibility and authority with others working with the court or the wider public.

In the second type of case, the magistrate's involvement could bring benefits both to the organization and to the magistracy itself. It would benefit the organization by enabling him or her to explain magistrates' interests and expectations in situations where the organization has dealings with the court; and it could help the bench to gain a better understanding of the organization, where that is relevant, and of the opportunities and constraints in the work with which it is engaged. There is anecdotal evidence that if members of a visiting committee saw that their prison was coming under severe pressure from overcrowding, they could use their influence on judicial colleagues to restrain the use of custodial remands and prison sentences.

The third situation is where the magistrate acts in a position of authority and responsibility, for example as a facilitator for a restorative conference, or as a chair, moderator or mediator for a process of community resolution. That situation is more complex. There will normally be principles, rules and guidance concerning the way in which the function should be performed, and the person acting in that role will usually have been trained in understanding and applying them. This is an area where new ideas and new ways of doing things are being constantly developed, and rules and protocols for accountability and legitimacy are being created alongside them. As Aubrey Fox points out, magistrates should not be excluded from this process and could make an important contribution to it, both as magistrates and as citizens, but rules and understandings, including understandings about their accountability, will need to be established.

Concerns and Considerations

A magistrate taking part in activities of the kind discussed in this brief introduction would clearly be required to declare his or her interest on appointment or when starting the activity concerned, and also when a person encountered in the course of that activity had previously appeared before the magistrate in court, or did so subsequently, in which case the magistrate would not take part in the proceedings. A particular issue for any expansion of the role which magistrates might play in 'providing' organizations would be the possible conflict of interest where the organization has a commercial interest in the effect of decisions which magistrates take in court. The issue would need especially careful consideration if, as must be expected, more justice-related activities are outsourced to the private or voluntary sector and become subject to payment by results.

More generally, a significant expansion would inevitably involve serious questions of selection to ensure that magistrates had the time and motivation to do justice to the responsibilities involved, and were not limited to retired or semi-retired members of the middle-class and those who were relatively better off. Kate Green (in *Chapter 9*) and Howard Riddle (in *Chapter 15*) raise those questions: there is no single or obvious answer but they make some suggestions and some resolution is clearly needed.

Magistrates would also need to be seen, and see themselves, as members of the same wider community as those with whom their work brought them into contact. That is, or should be, the essence of community justice. It does not require them to be members of the same social class or ethnic group, so long as the membership of the magistracy as a whole is reasonably diverse, but it does require that they should not be seen to be controlling or punishing a separate and in some way alien or threatening class of people who tend to be treated as less than full citizens or full members of the community, with the difficulties that presents for them in exercising their rights and especially their responsibilities.

Conclusions

The roads starting from the crossroads seem to lead in three directions.

One points towards the magistracy continuing more or less as at present, with some further improvements in efficiency and probably a stronger framework of central direction and guidance.

Another points to the magistrates' courts taking an increasing volume of the work which now goes to the Crown Court, with a greater emphasis on professionalisation and perhaps eventually within a unified court system as suggested in the Auld Report (Auld, 2001).

The third is in the direction of developing some of the forms of community justice described in this introduction.

The first two might have more appeal to government as being 'tidy' and easier to control but they offer an uncertain future for the lay magistracy. The third has the risks which have been indicated above, but it provides more opportunities for innovation and a role which might be more vital and rewarding both for magistrates and for the communities they serve. In the final chapter, Howard Riddle speaks for all the contributors in acknowledging that improvements are needed, but he expresses pride in the country's system of summary justice and confidence that magistrates will remain at its heart.

Endnotes

---

1. The word 'deliver' is now taken for granted as part of the language of government and management, but it is more suited to products or commodities that can be bought and sold than it is to justice and the work of the courts.

References

Auld, Sir Robin (2001), *A Review of the Criminal Courts of England and Wales*, London: The Stationery Office.

Ministry of Justice (2007), *Evaluation of the North Liverpool Community Justice Centre*, Ministry of Justice Research Series, 12/07, London: Ministry of Justice.

Ministry of Justice (2011), *The Strengths and Skills of the Judiciary in the Magistrates' Courts*, Ministry of Justice Research Series, 9/11, London: Ministry of Justice.

1

MAGISTRATES AND THE RIGHT TO A FAIR TRIAL

Andrew Ashworth is the Vinerian Professor of English Law at the University of Oxford, and writes on criminal law, sentencing, and human rights. He was a member (1999-2007) and then chairman (2007-2010) of the Sentencing Advisory Panel, and in the 1980s and early 1990s was a member of the team that produced the first set of Magistrates' Association Sentencing Guidelines.

MAGISTRATES AND THE RIGHT TO A FAIR TRIAL

Andrew Ashworth

Whatever happens to the magistracy in the next decade or two, it is axiomatic that magistrates' courts must be able to provide a fair trial for cases appropriate to their jurisdiction. That is a human right (according to Article 6 of the European Convention on Human Rights), but its significance is sometimes smudged and sometimes overlooked. The talk about community justice is fine — can lay magistrates provide that, as they were always supposed to? Or do we need some kind of 'neighbourhood resolution panel' to ensure that the real 'community' is in touch with the administration of criminal justice? Well, I would say that we need to assess all these possibilities by reference to the idea of a fair trial. Thus, according to Article 6(1) the 'fair hearing' which is the right of all defendants must take place before an 'independent and impartial tribunal'. Or, if it does not, the defendant must be able, as of right, to insist that the case comes before such a tribunal. That, in law and in good sense, is no less important than whether the composition of the tribunal represents 'the community' properly.

The idea of a fair trial is not confined to the actual proceedings. One pressing question is how cases are allocated. In an ideal world, perhaps, the most serious cases would go to the Crown Court; cases of moderate seriousness would come before the magistrates' courts; and there would be a lower tier of out-of-court disposals, cases that do not really need to come before a court.

There is understandable concern about the lowest tier: the simplification of criminal justice is a worthy objective, and in days of austerity a cheaper alternative has some attractions (so long as there are no perverse incentives operating here). But the lowest tier needs close examination, as Rod Morgan argues in his contribution in *Chapter 12*. There is an immediate danger at this level, which is that those who are handing out the penalties do not have any judicial role — indeed many of them are police officers, whose role is to keep the peace and to investigate crime, not to adjudicate or to engage in 'sentencing'. The Crown Prosecution Service now see some cases, and may advise on simple cautions as well as conditional cautions. But penalty notices for disorder can be and are handed out by police officers, not only for offences of public disorder but also for some offences of theft and of criminal damage. The possibility of refusing a PND and suggesting to the police officer that a prosecution should be brought is theoretical, but one wonders how often it is used. It is vital for the right to a fair trial, since a person must be able to challenge a penalty in front of a court. But if it is not really practical …?

Concern about police officers performing a sentencing function by handing out PNDs is not the only issue here. There are also standards of proportionality and consistency. Proportionality here has at least two stages. First, is the penalty for a PND offence (which may be theft from a shop) satisfactory, and comparable with what a court might give in the circumstances? Secondly, does the penalty take sufficient account of the person's means? The usual answer to this is that PNDs are rough-and-ready (justified by speed and simplicity) and cannot be adjusted to means, and that many of the penalties are low enough to be paid by anyone. But that is questionable when the penalty is £80. So we need more discussion of proportionality here, and some reconsideration of whether PNDs should be available for thefts at all. Then there is the consistency question. Of course one can demonstrate that magistrates' courts in different areas seem to have different rates of using certain sentences (for example imprisonment, community sentences) which have not been flattened out by the sentencing guidelines. But, irrespective of that, it is important to ask what steps are being taken to ensure that police officers and the CPS pursue a consistent policy in relation to the out-of-court disposals which they may use. Other people may discuss local accountability and the role of the 'community' (I have so far resisted adding, whatever that means); but issues of fairness, proportionality and consistency must not be overlooked.

I say nothing more here about the allocation of cases between the Crown Court and magistrates' courts (although it seems that the arguments about trials for theft are to be re-visited in the near future), but there is one sensitive aspect of fair trials that must be raised. One reason why governments have mostly been concerned to transfer types of case from the Crown Court down to the magistrates' courts is that they are cheaper and quicker. But, swimming against the tide, I wonder whether magistrates should not place more emphasis on reducing the speed of their justice and ensuring that proceedings give a greater impression of rounded consideration. Now this is not an allegation, because I have no up-to-date evidence either way, and courts differ across the country. But large surveys done some years ago suggested time and again that defendants and their lawyers prefer the Crown Court because they regard the quality of justice as better: they think they have a better opportunity to put their case, and they think their case receives fuller consideration. Now that does not mean that we should increase the use of jury trials. But, in terms of the appearance of justice and the quality of justice, it may give rise to a little reflection on whether (some) magistrates' courts should revisit their procedures and the messages that they may send out, particularly in trials and in remand hearings.

Despite the pressures of time, the appearance of haste quickly becomes the appearance of unfairness, and of 'summary justice' at its worst. Would I be entirely wrong to suggest that the lay magistracy should promote themselves more as a fair way of dealing with cases than as an economical way? If magistrates are to garner support for their still-central position in the criminal justice system, should that not be done on the basis of a re-invigoration of standards of fairness (and the appearance of fairness)?

2

THE MAGISTRACY — A PROFESSIONAL COURT?

Louis Blom-Cooper QC was called to the Bar by Middle Temple in July 1952 and practised until 2004, He took silk in 1970, Throughout his career he engaged in the campaign for the abolition of capital punishment and the abolition of the mandatory life sentence for murder. From 1966-1978 he was a member of the Home Secretary's Advisory Council on the Penal System, and chaired that council's report in June 1978 on Sentences of Imprisonment.

THE MAGISTRACY — A PROFESSIONAL COURT?

Louis Blom-Cooper

Of all the criminal trials that take place in the magistrates' courts of England and Wales (which constitute 95 per cent of all trials in the criminal courts) less than ten per cent are tried by individual district judges (formerly, stipendiary magistrates) of whom, in 2010, there were 143 lawyers sitting full-time and 151 lawyers sitting part-time. As professional lawyers aspiring to judicial preferment they are recruited and trained separately; they are culturally distinct from the 26,000 or so lay magistrates who sit in panels of three to try the 95 per cent of less serious criminal cases. Generally speaking, there are no mixed criminal tribunals for adult offenders, composed of district judges and magistrates. Justices of the peace (to give the lay magistrates their ancient title) are drawn from all walks of life, with little or no qualification in the processes of judicial behaviour. Together with initial training and in-service tuition, many of them readily bring to the magistracy the professionalism of their separate fields of endeavour. Yet there is no formal judicial link between the justice of the peace and the district judge.

Although not disqualified from appointment to the lay bench of the magistracy, lawyers are an uncommon sight among those sitting in judgment. Even those lawyers engaged in legal practice (including conceivably a member of Queen's Counsel, no less) may exceptionally be appointed; the only restriction is that they cannot appear as counsel in the courts where they might be asked to sit in judgement. That such a legally qualified magistrate might find himself or herself exceptionally adjudicating on a case conducted by a close fellow practitioner could be avoided by instant disqualification from sitting. The odd occasion in which a legal practitioner would be one of three magistrates seems rarely to have aroused public (let alone specialist) interest, a suggestion for emulation on a regular basis has gone unheard, even unnoticed beyond the instant case.

I make these prefatory remarks as an introduction to a personal experience. From 1966 until 1981 I was that *rara avis*—a practising member of the English Bar, called by Middle Temple in 1952, becoming a Queen's Counsel in 1970, practising largely in the field of public law, at a time when the concept of judicial review of ministerial decisions was developing as a major feature of civil litigation. But I anticipate my magisterial experience by describing the route to magisterial status. The description reveals the nature of the legal profession at that time and its resistance to change, either in the form of a unified system for solicitors and barristers or for a lessening of the marked difference in the attitudes of the legally-qualified and those not versed in the ways of those fortunately imbued with the notion of the superior status of all English common lawyers.

When I began my career at the Bar, unlike my contemporaries in practice, I acquired no experience, let alone any expertise in the practice of the criminal law. I saw nothing of the daily fare of a magistrates' court, although I had an academic interest in the criminal process as it functioned forensically and in its investigatory powers. Thus, extra-murally and extra-curricularly, I had some pretensions towards the study of criminology, and more particularly the penal system. In the 1950s, until the abolition in 1965 of the death penalty for murder, I was actively engaged in the campaign for its abolition (homicide has remained a perennial interest). It was as a part-time academic—I began teaching criminology to social science students in the Department of Social Administration at Bedford College, University of London — that I touched base with the members of the Magistrates' Association. Kindly, I was invited to give talks to groups of magistrates up and down the country on topics that encompassed the field of crime and justice (including the punishment of offenders). I was quickly made aware of the fact that I might possess some legal acumen (of a distinctly academic variety) but I was hopelessly out of touch with the pressing problems of a magistracy that was involved daily in dispensing justice as it was experienced in the courtroom. The oft-repeated comment — nearly always delivered in a friendly manner — was that, interesting as some of my remarks were, I saw the magisterial dilemma of doing justice to the public interest and the individual defendant only through tinted spectacles. It determined me to rectify the omission, were I to continue my lecturing activities.

There was another aspect to my desire to rectify my lopsided view of the criminal process as it unfolded in the magistrates' (and other) courts. The ambition among practitioners was generally to round off their career at the Bar (either criminal or civil) by becoming judges, if not on the top rung of the judicial ladder at least in what were, until 1971, the Assize Courts (now Crown Courts) or, more relevant to my career, in the civil courts where judging, not by way of trial by judge and jury, was the process of finding the facts and applying the law. Yet the avenue of advancement into the judiciary provided, at that time at least, little experience of being a decision-maker. On the magisterial bench, the magistrate is the decision-maker of the factual matrix as well as conducting the process of determining guilt and punishment. Even today, the lawyer aspiring to a judgeship will, almost invariably, have spent time acting as a part-time assistant recorder or recorder. As such he or she will *not* be a decision-maker but will generally only have experience of summing up the evidence to an expectant jury which deliberates and delivers its unarticulated verdict.

I had the good fortune and privilege to become acquainted with Gerald Gardiner, an outstanding lawyer who in 1964 became Lord Chancellor in the Labour administration of Harold Wilson. I asked him if he would be prepared to appoint me to the London magistracy. He applauded my wish to broaden my experience of the criminal law in action. I was duly appointed in 1966 and even allowed to dispense with the requirement to undergo initial training. If that was a proper concession to a practising lawyer like me, I now regret it. It is as necessary for the untutored to undergo initial training, whenever he or she comes into public life.

My first experience was sitting — at least in the early days — as a book-end at Greenwich and Woolwich Magistrates' Courts. I cannot vouch for any rejections my legally unqualified colleagues had of my presence. If they thought that the qualified lawyer was an unwelcome injection into a system designed to reflect a popular outlook on criminal justice, they were kind enough not to express any degree of animosity. The process of deliberation in the justices' retiring room was usually uneventful, although I suspect strongly that my unorthodox views on penal affairs did not always accord with those of other magistrates. But my recollection is that only rarely did we impose immediate terms of custody for convicted offenders, so that I was never troubled, and did not cause trouble. But I was conscious then (as I will explain later) of the relationship between the magistrates and the justices' clerks who served ostensibly as the court's legal advisers and judicial amanuenses. That experience was to await my translation in 1969 to the City of London Magistrates' Court sitting primarily in the Mansion House (the only building that combined an official residence for the mayor, a courtroom and prison cells in the basement). The change under the Justice of the Peace Act 1969 was truly innovative. Until then, for centuries, the elected aldermen of the City of London administered the criminal jurisdiction of the city. The change was the formation of a bench of 72 justices, of whom 24 were the extant aldermen. The arrangement of the municipally elected and the lay justices of the peace worked well enough. It seemed then, and appears now, to arouse little public concern, apart from the odd high-profile case.

It was not too long before I became, by virtue of seniority, the presiding magistrate for the day's working list. It was a peculiar feature of the City of London Magistrates' Court that by the manner of its composition, and the range of judicial fare, it provided an unusually high degree of professionalism in the performance of judicial duties in cases that reflected the criminality of a sparse residential population and a large daily peripatetic workforce at the heart of the country's financial services. An example of this unique mixture was the last case in which I was involved. I sat with two magistrates — one the leading liquidator and chairman of the Royal Opera House, the other (a woman) the head of the international section of Barclays Bank in the City of London.

The case was intrinsically unique. Under the Exchange Control Act 1947 (later repealed) there was an odd provision, that with the consent of the prosecutor and the accused, a magistrates' court could try an offence under the Act summarily. The monetary penalty on conviction could be up to five times the amount of money involved in the commission of the statutory offence. The case involved two stockbrokers who had engaged in a practice known in financial circles as a 'revolving-fund fraud'. The practice was to send monies whizzing around the world's financial markets, picking up in the process the dollar premium on the monies. The practice was criminal.

We sat for 30 working days; the prosecution was expertly conducted by Treasury counsel, who regularly appeared at the Central Criminal Court at the Old Bailey, and leading counsel for the two accused. At the end of the hearings, we reserved our judgment, later delivering a 45-page reasoned finding in support of a guilty verdict. We considered imprisonment unnecessary and fined the two offenders half a million pounds. We were told subsequently that, if the case had gone to the Old Bailey before a jury, it would have lasted anything up to six months. This instance of a mixed tribunal was cited approvingly by the Roskill Committee on Serious Fraud Trials in 1984 as an example of why the committee's recommendation for a professional tribunal in serious fraud cases should be adopted. After the election in 1997 the Labour administration tried legislatively to substitute a mixed tribunal for trial by jury in serious fraud cases. The provision in the Criminal Justice Act 2003 could be implemented only on a positive motion of Parliament. It failed. The rest is history; the silence betokens an unwavering popular devotion to the system of trial by judge and jury. But the day must surely come when the time taken and the escalating costs in serious (usually complex) cases will dictate a change. Will a revised magistracy play any part in such a development?

I must apologise after the single example I have given for pointing in the direction of a revamped magistracy by forging the link of the professional lawyer (the district judge) and the lay magistrate (the justice of the peace). The late Barbara Wootton, whose outstanding biography *A Critical Woman* was published in 2011,[1] once proclaimed that for any generalisation you need at least two examples. To avoid dilation on the topic of mixed tribunals, I record that I actually sat on a second 'revolving-fund fraud' trial on the City of London bench, and other multitudinous cases during my 12 years as a magistrate. I can say that I found the presence of two non-legally qualified magistrates almost invariably helpful, even on occasion a healthy corrective to my, seemingly excessive, liberal attitudes to criminal justice.

The one postscript for the magisterial experience I have described fortifies my plea for some development towards a mixed tribunal. At the end of the 30 day hearing I indicated to our justices' clerk (a man of huge experience and skill in managing a magistracy containing one or two mavericks and eccentrics) that we would be delivering a reasoned judgment, at which he metaphorically threw up his hands in horror, attesting a warning that that would be a recipe for disaster, because the accused (if found guilty) would appeal to the Central Criminal Court (strictly a rehearing before a circuit judge and two magistrates from the London magistracy). I politely pointed out that if we were wrong in our reasoned judgment, we jolly well ought to be appealed. In fact there was no appeal; the two stockbrokers were later struck off the list at the Stock Exchange.

The reaction of the justices' clerk was typical of the view at the time, that magistrates should decide cases and not open their mouths, just like the mother whale advising her young that it is only when you begin to spout that you get harpooned. The day of the unarticulated verdict of a magistrates' court has long since passed, although I expect that 'ticking of boxes' does not suffice to meet the need for giving reasons. It may just be possible to advance reform as an alternative to trial by jury. We should recall that Sir Robin Auld in his *Review of the Criminal Courts* in 2001[2] recommended that defendants should be allowed to waive jury trial if they so wished. The alternative form of the mixed composition of a criminal court could become that alternative.

Endnotes

1. Oakley A (2011), *A Critical Woman: Barbara Wootton, Social Science and Public Policy in the Twentieth Century*, London: Bloomsbury.
2. Auld, Sir Robin (2001), *Review of the Criminal Courts of England and Wales, Report*, London: The Stationery Office.

3

THE FUTURE OF THE FAMILY MAGISTRACY

Audrey Damazer commenced her career in the Magistrates Courts Service in 1978 as a trainee legal adviser at Sutton Magistrates' Court. Prior to that, she worked in the probation service for a short time. After having worked in various courts in Greater London, she was appointed to lead the Inner London training unit for magistrates and staff. This involved working closely with the Inner London Branch of the Magistrates' Association and running conferences and training events for magistrates. In 1997 Audrey Damazar was appointed justices' clerk for the Inner London Family Panel, then based at Wells Street and assisted in the establishment of the first magistrates' court solely dedicated to family proceedings court work, and in 2003 was made the family justices' clerk for the London-wide family panel. She contributed to the design and delivery of the Human Rights Act 1998 training throughout England and Wales and was a co-author of *Human Rights and the Courts* (Hook: Waterside Press, 2003). She also assisted in the delivery of Public Law Outline Training to the judiciary and the Judicial Studies Board's *Family Bench Book* as well as assisting with the Adoption and Children Act 2002 training and being on the working party looking at the authorisation of family and youth court justices. In her spare time she sits as a tribunal judge in the Social Entitlement Chamber (see http://www.justice.gov.uk/about/hmcts/tribunals).

THE FUTURE OF THE FAMILY MAGISTRACY

Audrey Damazar

As an individual who has worked alongside magistrates for nearly 30 years, I have never ceased to be struck by the diversity of skills and knowledge that is brought to the judicial decision-making process. In the family proceedings courts this has proved to be invaluable in a forum where open-mindedness, an understanding of child development and attachment theories and the needs of children are required. Every child is different, every family is different and although some of us may not have children we have all been a child and have experiences of growing up. We all have a different understanding of what a family is based on, our own experiences and cultural developments which have taken place over the years.

Since capital punishment was abolished, in some ways the decisions made in the family proceedings courts are the most draconian and life-changing which can be taken by any court in the United Kingdom. The decision whether to remove a child from its mother against a backdrop of belief that every child has a right to be brought up by their natural parent is a very difficult and also an emotional one, which can stay with the magistrate for a long time. I am not saying that the decision as to guilt or innocence in a criminal court is easier but in the family court the magistrates are looking at what is best for the child based on the evidence before the court: what is best for the child for the rest of their childhood. The decision requires a balancing of risk: will the child suffer more harm if she or he remains in the family or more harm if removed from the only family unit she or he has ever known.

The magistracy often sees the professional judiciary as a threat to its role. There is a perception in some areas that more and more work is allocated to the district judge (magistrates' courts). However I believe that we should see the professional judiciary as a key component in the continued existence of the magistracy in the family courts for the reasons I outline below.

The family justice system is very high on the political agenda at the moment due to concern about the numbers of children in the care system and the perceived delays in concluding cases before the courts. No one can disagree with the fact that there are areas which can be addressed for the benefit of children who appear in our courts. At the moment all public law proceedings start in the family proceeding courts. Due to the serious nature of the decisions required to be taken there is a groundswell of opinion that these decisions should only be made by the 'professional' judiciary.

The Family Justice Review published in 2011[1] proposes greater specialism of those who adjudicate on family matters but there is also agreement that a diet of only family work can be too stressful for any one person to carry. As I have outlined above there are incredibly difficult and emotional decisions which have to be made. I think there is a very strong argument to be made in this jurisdiction for three individuals being able to arrive at the best decision for the child. Knowledge of case law, statute and evidence are not the only requirements to ensure a sound decision. Understanding of the needs of the child, its developmental milestones along with an ability to be able to identify the key issues to be adjudicated on are essentials which in my view can best be met by a magistrate working closely with a judge.

I believe that the ideal judicial forum is a judge sitting with two magistrates. In other jurisdictions such as the Tribunals Service, with which I am familiar, when deciding on matters such as the claimant's ability to take care of themselves (disability living allowance) the tribunal judge sits with a qualified medical member and a disability member (someone with experience of working with or caring for a disabled person). Both of the lay members receive a fee and will sit on a far more regular basis than magistrates do at the moment. The tribunal judge as the professional judge ensures that the law is correctly applied and that a structured approach is applied to the decision-making process. This is in my view the ideal decision-making body in respect of family matters. Family law has become increasingly complex over the years with the introduction of the Children Act 1989, Adoption and Children Act 2002, the Human Rights Act 1998 and the growth in case law. There is no guarantee that such a tribunal will have the effect of reducing delays but judges on the whole are able to be more robust when dealing with applications for adjournments and further assessments; one of the main causes of delays in the family courts.

The Family Justice Review has proposed a single point of entry with gate-keeping teams undertaking the allocation of work under the direction of the designated family judge. Within the proposals greater emphasis is placed on the designated family judge who has been identified as the person who will locally manage the new Family Court. I am fearful that if we continue as we are we will see less public law work and greater private law work placed before the magistracy. My concerns are not based on territorial issues but a belief that magistrates reach sound decisions and have a key role to play in the delivery of family justice. I also believe that a mix of tribunal can only be for the better of children before our courts and ensure a more rounded approach to the issues including of where the child's needs can be best met.

I think that the time has also come for us to revisit the voluntary nature of the magistracy. Within family law it has become more and more difficult to cover the essential legal knowledge and competences within the time allotted for training. Greater reliance has had to be placed on magistrates studying in their own time and attending more local training to ensure sufficient knowledge and understanding to carry out their role. More and more individuals have full-time jobs and there is reluctance on the part of employers to provide the time off to sit and to attend training. I believe that society has a different view of public service to that held in the last century. It is becoming more and more difficult to ensure that we have a diverse panel of family justices not only for the reasons set out above but also because of the time required to read all the papers which often has to be done in their own time. The job market has changed, if we want individuals who have a positive contribution to make to the family justice system, consideration needs to be given to paying individuals for their time. If they are to work alongside judges, the valuable contribution which can be made by individuals who are not trained lawyers but have knowledge, experience and understanding of families and the resources available to support families to meet the needs of their children must be acknowledged and valued.

I sincerely hope that the magistracy will continue to play a key role in the delivery of family justice. The family justice system is facing fundamental change over the next few years and the magistracy has a responsibility to ensure that the changes allow for magistrates to contribute to the complex decision-making process and thereby ensure the best outcomes for children who appear before our courts.

Endnotes

1. Norgrove D (2011), *Family Justice Review: Final Report,* London: Ministry of Justice and Department for Education; and also Cardiff: Welsh Government.

4

PROMOTING INNOVATION:
HOW THE MAGISTRACY CAN MAKE A DIFFERENCE

Aubrey Fox is the Director of Strategic Planning at the Center for Court Innovation (USA). In November 2011, he launched the Centre for Justice Innovation, an institution that seeks to promote thoughtful criminal justice reform in the UK by focusing on the use of demonstration projects. Prior to that, he was Project Director of Bronx Community Solutions, a one-of-its-kind initiative launched in January 2005 that seeks to meet the ambitious goal of changing a large and tradition-bound public agency's approach to low-level crime. He was responsible for the day-to-day leadership of 20 administrators, social workers and community service crew supervisors charged with providing increased sentencing options for 11,000 non-violent criminal offenders a year. Aubrey Fox graduated with a master's degree in public policy from the University of California at Berkeley, served as a VISTA Volunteer in San Antonio, Texas, and was a Warren Weaver Fellow at the Rockefeller Foundation and a member of Coro's Leadership New York programme. His work has appeared in *Newsday*, the *Gotham Gazette, Judicature, Justice System Journal, Court Review* and other places. He is co-author of *Trial and Error in Criminal Justice Reform: Learning from Failure* (Washington DC: Urban Institute Press, 2010).

PROMOTING INNOVATION:
HOW THE MAGISTRACY CAN MAKE A DIFFERENCE

Aubrey Fox

This chapter seeks to provide a series of practical tips for magistrates who want to promote new models of problem-solving innovation. It reviews some of the lessons learned from the work of the USA-based Center for Court Innovation in helping criminal justice practitioners implement, evaluate and disseminate model projects.

In his *Introduction*, David Faulkner outlines a key challenge faced by the magistracy. As he writes, a top-down central government bureaucracy with an aversion to risk-taking has stifled innovation and experimentation at a local level. To counter these trends, Faulkner argues that, for magistrates, a 'promising area of exploration may be the various forms of "community" or "neighbourhood" justice', where important developments are taking place and there is a strong case for reform.

This chapter uses this observation as a jumping-off point. Its perspective is essentially optimistic: while media attention focuses on policy clashes in Westminster, underneath the radar, local practitioners across England and Wales have launched demonstration projects in response to specific, local, criminal justice problems. With their connections to local communities, magistrates are positioned to be leaders in encouraging this kind of innovation — both inside and outside of the courtroom.

To be sure, there are downsides to this type of approach. It can be time-consuming and painstaking, and favours incremental reform as opposed to wholesale change. Yet there is ample evidence that demonstration projects are capable of both solving local problems and generating knowledge with the potential to transform the wider field of criminal justice. In England and Wales, this has included specialist domestic violence courts, drug courts, mental health courts, intensive alternative to custody projects and new models of integrated offender management.

What lessons can be derived from these new innovations in criminal justice for those interested in strengthening the magistracy?

Magistrates Matter

The first lesson is in some respects obvious, yet worth reviewing in light of the ongoing debate about what role magistrates play in encouraging compliance with court orders and public trust in the law. One of the most fascinating findings coming out of the latest round of research into drug courts in the United States is the key role played by judges in their success. A new study of nearly two dozen drug courts conducted by the Urban Institute, the Center for Court Innovation (New York) and the Research Triangle Institute found that 18 months after admission into drug courts, participants reported decreased drug use and 50 per cent fewer criminal acts than a comparison group. Notably, the study showed that the strongest predictor of reduced future criminality was a defendant's attitude towards the judge. Having positive perceptions of the judge was also the greatest predictor of reduced drug use and reduced violations of supervision.[1] The judicial role is a powerful one. A message communicated by a judge or a magistrate may have more impact than the same message conveyed by a probation officer or a social worker.

Pay Attention to Process

The research into drug courts showed reduced criminality among defendants who perceived the judge to have treated them fairly and respectfully — even those defendants with extensive prior criminal histories and those who had received unfavourable sentences. This suggests a possibly counter-intuitive conclusion that how litigants view the justice system is more tied to the perceived fairness of the process than to its outcome — in other words, they care more about fairness than whether they 'win' or 'lose' their case.[2] In addition, evidence suggests that defendants are more likely to comply with court orders if they perceive the process as fair.

Little Things Can Make a Big Difference

One encouraging implication of the research cited above is that even small changes in how courts operate can lead to big improvements — although they may in some cases challenge customs of how English courtrooms typically operate. Some of the practices that appear to be consistent with improved perceptions of fairness include having magistrates address defendants by name, using plain English and avoiding jargon in court sessions, engaging defendants in dialogue about their case and minimising waiting times. Magistrates can also call on other players in the courtroom for help — for example, working with court administrators to rethink how courtroom rules are posted, explained and enforced in a way that is clear and respectful, and encouraging defence representatives to ensure that defendants know the status of their case and what is required for compliance with court orders.

Look for Inspiration

Magistrates can look to examples of their colleagues across the Atlantic who have launched demonstration projects that have had far-reaching implications for the criminal justice system. One example can be found in Hawaii, where in 2004 Judge Stephen Alm started a programme he called HOPE

(Hawaii's Opportunity Probation with Enforcement). HOPE was aimed at drug-addicted probationers at risk of violating the terms of their probation mandate. Alm noticed in his first week on the job that probation officers were routinely waiting until 20 or more violations had occurred before returning the case to court. With HOPE, probationers are regularly drug-tested, and if they fail their tests are given an immediate and certain, but short, two-day jail sentence as a sanction. Research shows that the programme has significantly reduced crime and probation revocations, and therefore prison costs, while reducing failed drug tests and missed probation appointments.

Start Small

One factor that helped Alm was that he started small with 34 participants in a single courtroom in Oahu. This allowed him to test the concept before expanding operations. Not only does this limit the need for extra funding but perhaps, more importantly, starting small provided Judge Alm with the opportunity to work out the kinks of the model. Equally importantly, it avoided the potential for overwhelming the system with sudden demands for drug-testing and immediate penalties for failed drug tests. Starting small and engaging in a rigorous trial-and-error process is crucial to the ultimate success of demonstration projects. And the humble origins of HOPE have hardly limited its success: today nearly one in five probationers in Oahu is supervised under HOPE, and the programme is being replicated throughout the country with the support of the United States Department of Justice.

Capitalise on the Symbolic Authority of Magistrates

One of the key drivers of problem-solving innovation in the United States has been the so-called 'symbolic' authority of the judge. Judges have played a key role in generating resources and marshalling support for new initiatives like drug courts.[3] As part-time volunteers, magistrates in England and Wales may be somewhat more limited in their power to effect change, and as David Faulkner notes, many 'have been inhibited from becoming engaged in activities outside the court setting'. Yet the fact that they are not full-time professionals may in reality be an advantage: as respected members of the community, they bring an independent set of connections, relationships, and expertise to the table. One example can be found in London, where magistrate David Chesterton serves as the chair of the Young Offenders Academy, a new project meant to change how the criminal justice system engages young people. While presumably not all magistrates would be interested in playing that kind of advocacy and fundraising role, it seems likely that a significant minority of the roughly 26,000 magistrates in England and Wales might—provided they are given the right kind of encouragement and support.

'Kick the Tyres' (Test it Out)

Another way magistrates can become more involved in problem-solving justice is to conduct site visits. For example, a magistrate could visit a community payback project or drug rehabilitation programme to see how they work. This would have at least two benefits: first, it would help magistrates to learn more about what happens outside of the courtroom, and second, it would communicate a message to local partners that magistrates care about how these programmes operate.

Demand Accountability

A key role played by judges involved in problem-solving courts in the United States has been to ensure accountability with programme conditions. For example, the Harlem Parole Re-entry Court works with adult offenders released from prison under parole (the equivalent of probation in England and Wales) supervision who are returning to the Harlem neighbourhood of Manhattan. Participants are required to return to the re-entry court frequently to meet with case managers and parole officers, and to appear before an administrative law judge, who closely monitors their compliance with their parole conditions. Closer to home, in places like Cardiff, magistrates play a key role in supervising offenders on drug rehabilitation requirements, meeting with them on a monthly basis, while in Bradford (and until recently) Leeds, magistrates regularly review the progress of offenders assigned to intensive community orders. While spreading these kinds of practices more widely may require legislative change (currently, only magistrates and judges in certain areas of the country are given this authority), magistrates might look for opportunities to expand their ability to review compliance with court orders post-sentencing.

Don't Go it Alone

One of the lessons learned about successful demonstration projects is the role external champions often play in helping local practitioners obtain needed political support or funding. For example, in recent years, the English charity Co-ordinated Action Against Domestic Abuse (CAADA) has provided critical support to practitioners throughout England and Wales working with victims of domestic violence. CAADA has helped government officials launch Multi-Agency Risk Assessment Conferences (MARACs), which bring together the police, probation, health and other local charities to create safety plans for high risk victims, and provide training to independent domestic violence advisers, who support the MARACs. All told, there are 240 MARACs operating in England and Wales, and CAADA has provided accredited training to over 1,100 independent domestic violence advisers. Interestingly, champions like CAADA have tended to come from outside government, which points to the role that credible intermediary organizations can play in aiding local practitioners and promoting innovation more broadly. This suggests that magistrates (both locally and its national representative organization) would be well served to try to link up with such bodies.

Magistrates Are Credible Supporters of Demonstration Projects

Most sustainable projects recognise the need to remain apolitical in their leadership and to reach out to all parties, not just those in office when a project is favoured. Political support is often temporary and can be reliant on relationships that can end unexpectedly and rarely exceed the duration of a project. The politics of a project can go wrong when that scheme becomes too closely tied to the fortunes of incumbent politicians, and therefore vulnerable to termination or funding cuts if the political landscape changes. For all these reasons, magistrates can be useful allies of demonstration projects. They can provide apolitical and credible support for schemes that are meant to improve the administration of justice and promote widely shared outcomes like increased compliance with court orders or reduced re-offending. One example is the intensive community order (ICO) programme, a seven-site pilot project launched by the Ministry of Justice in 2009 that is meant to give magistrates a credible alternative to a short-term (typically one year or less) prison sentence.[4] Although central government is no longer providing financial support to the pilot areas, the seven sites continue to operate ICO projects, which have achieved some promising early results (and report that magistrates are very satisfied with the scheme). Magistrates can offer key support to ICOs in the pilot areas, as well as helping to spread the word about the success of the model to other parts of England and Wales.

Demonstration projects are not the only path to change in criminal justice. There will always be a place for legislation, central government policymaking and large-scale structural reforms. Yet without much fanfare or publicity, practitioners in England and Wales have had a good record in recent years of stimulating change from the ground up.

Perhaps the single unifying theme of this chapter is the role magistrates can play in encouraging more of this type of positive change in criminal justice. The challenge for magistrates is ensuring that they are at the front of and central to these developments. The United States offers a constructive example: at a recent community justice conference in Washington DC, roughly 20 per cent of attendees came from the judiciary—a remarkable proportion given that the tradition of judicial independence has often discouraged those who pass sentences from participating in these kinds of events. To be sure, this did not happen overnight (for example, the first problem-solving court was opened in Dade County, Florida in 1989), but it is an enormously positive development for the field. Increasing the proportion of magistrates who participate in similar events in England and Wales would be a similarly positive development.

Endnotes

1. For a more complete summary of the study, see http://www.courtinnovation.org/sites/default/files/documents/MADCE_PP.pdf.

2. The key elements of so-called 'procedural justice', as defined by academic experts like Tom Tyler of Yale University and Mike Hough of the University of London, include giving litigants (this includes victims and other courtroom users in addition to defendants) the opportunity to tell their story, a sense that they are respected, an understanding of what went on in court and a belief that the decision-making process itself is unbiased and trustworthy. See also, Faulkner D and Burnett R (2012), *Where Next for Criminal Justice?*, Chapters 1 and 7, Bristol: Policy Press.

3. For a more extensive discussion of the symbolic authority of judges, see Carol Fisler, Greg Berman and Aubrey Fox, 'Risks and Rewards: Drug Courts and Community Reintegration', *National Drug Court Institute Review*, Vol. III, 2. Available at http://www.courtinnovation.org/pdf/drugcourt_reintegration.pdf.

4. The programme is also known by its original name, 'Intensive Alternatives to Custody': see Ministry of Justice (2011), *Evaluation of Intensive Alternatives to Custody Pilots*, Research Summary, 3/11, London: Ministry of Justice.

5

THE LINCHPIN OF THE JUSTICE SYSTEM

Frances Gibb has been a newspaper journalist for more than 30 years. She is currently Legal Editor of *The Times*, a position she has held since 2000. Before that she was that newspaper's legal correspondent, from 1982. Her previous posts include being a general reporter on *The Times* and Art Sales Correspondent with the *Daily Telegraph*. She was a trainee on *The Times Higher Education Correspondent* for four years. Frances Gibb is currently a governor of King's College School, Wimbledon, since 2005, with responsibility for the arts, senior school and she is a volunteer at Abbeyfield House, New Malden (a care home which deals with the elderly and mentally infirm). She was married for 31 years to Joseph Cahill, a surgeon, who died in 2009. She has three grown-up sons and her interests include the theatre, gardening and her family.

THE LINCHPIN OF THE JUSTICE SYSTEM

Frances Gibb

Their official title, justices of the peace, seems like something from another age. But is our lay magistracy similarly time-expired?

As magistrates celebrate 650 years, they remain the cornerstone of the justice system in that they are responsible for 90 per cent or more of cases going through the criminal or civil courts. Yet despite that central role, their mood in recent months has seemed less than upbeat. One hundred of their courts have been closed and their workload has dropped dramatically. Tens of thousands of cases that they used to handle are dealt with instead by out-of-court penalties, handed out by police or prosecutors. So, in the words of John Fassenfelt, the chairman of the Magistrates' Association, they are feeling 'unloved, unappreciated'.[1]

Things have been worse. When Jack Straw became Lord Chancellor in 2007, the association feared that he was gunning for the lay magistracy. Straw attacked them for clogging up the Crown Court by sending thousands of trivial cases there that, he said, they could deal with themselves. The Lord Chancellor, who was also Justice Secretary, had form: some years earlier, as Home Secretary, he commissioned a study into their role, after criticism that they were slow and inconsistent. The Home Office believed that they should be phased out over time and replaced with paid professionals, or full-time district judges.

Nor has the threat entirely receded: the Ministry of Justice published a report in the autumn of 2011[2] on the relative merits of the lay and salaried bench. What did it find? First, that magistrates were perceived to have a greater connection with the local community than do district judges and so were better placed to dispense 'local justice'. They were also associated with fairness: some felt that a bench of three had a greater degree of democracy than a single judge; and also that they were more likely to be 'open-minded' and less 'case-hardened' or 'fatigued'. And, of course, they are not paid. District judges, on the other hand, were praised for their speed in handling cases and legal expertise. Average case hearings were shorter and they were felt to be better at managing cases.

So a mixed bag. But there is certainly no suggestion within the realms of policy-makers that, on the strength of these findings, JPs should be phased out. Quite the contrary. With the present financial pressures, the benefits of an unpaid magistracy are obvious. The riots of last summer also drove home to ministers the benefits of swift summary justice. So while magistrates may be feeling unloved, at the time of writing, ministers plan to put them back where they ought to be—at the heart of the community. The idea is to build on lessons of the riots and speed up cases going through the courts with more evening and early morning sittings. Magistrates might have a bigger role overseeing the handing out of fixed penalties so that fewer cases would be diverted from the justice system.

At the same time, ministers want to find ways to devolve up to 70,000 cases a year from the Crown Court to magistrates. Whether that can be done without encroaching on a defendant's right to elect jury trial remains to be seen. But Fassenfelt makes a strong case:

> If you want to save money, then why allow all these cases to go to the Crown Court?

And freeing up the latter, where cases take many months to come to trial, would enable swifter justice for murders, rapes and serous assaults.

So all is far from gloomy. And not least because in recent years, magistrates have upped their lobbying power. Time was when the Magistrates' Association was little more than that, a quiet body that existed as a focal point for members but had little to do with the media. Now it regularly has dealings with the press: a run of high-profile feisty chairmen and women have ensured headlines on controversial proposals from respective governments and no longer is their voice heard only behind scenes. Magistrates have learnt that they do have clout and can effect change.

Undoubtedly the Constitutional Reform Act 2005 made a big impact. This paved the way for magistrates—their training, recruitment and discipline—to be brought into the judicial family, coming officially under the aegis of the Lord Chief Justice. It has given them a direct line to senior judges and seen senior judges, in turn, speak out for their lay judicial colleagues. So a group that is not far off 27,000-strong in England and Wales is beginning at least to punch its weight.

If, though, bigger waves are being made with the politicians and the media, what of magistrates' impact among the general public? The old image of magistrates' courts as 'police' courts presided over by women in hats may have gone but people still view JPs as likely to side with prosecutors—hence the numbers of defendants who elect trial by judge and jury, in cases where they can. Magistrates are also still seen as middle-class, predominantly white and female. Young working-class men and particularly those from the ethnic minority communities may not always think that they will get a fair hearing. The reality is that there are almost equal numbers of men and women, but they appear to remain overwhelmingly middle-class and conservative. Huge efforts have been made to recruit younger JPs and those from non-professional backgrounds and more than eight per cent are now drawn from the ethnic minorities. But not in London—where the percentage of black magistrates is below that in the general population.[3] And with increasing demands on magistrates' time in terms of training, it remains difficult to persuade employers to give people time off: two fifths of magistrates are retired.

All this makes it harder to promote the importance of the role of magistrates in dispensing local justice. It should not detract from it, though. Magistrates need to change their demographic if they want to maintain and increase public confidence in their courts and that will take continuing and sustained public relations efforts. Meanwhile, they also need — as their leaders seem keen to do — to leave aside battles on court closures and focus on more flexible working arrangements, new locations for hearings and other reforms to improve summary justice. But in their increased professionalism, in improved media and political relations and in efforts to reach out to the community through open events and recruitment drives, JPs can undoubtedly claim credit. It remains work in progress. But the value of magistrates' role, as volunteers who form the linchpin of the justice system, is not in doubt.

Endnotes

1. 'Unloved and underworked: Why JPs need a morale boost'. Interview with John Fassenfelt by Francis Gibb, *The Times*, January 19th, 2012.
2. *The Strengths and Skills of the Judiciary in the Magistrates' Courts* (2011), Research Series, 9/11, London: Ministry of Justice.
3. Source Ministry of Justice database showing 'Serving magistrates by HMCS Region, England and Wales', as at March 31st, 2011. These and other published statistics are available at the Judiciary website: see http://www.judiciary.gov.uk/publications-and-reports/statistics/magistrates-statistics

6

PROBATION AND THE MAGISTRACY:
A NEW RELATIONSHIP FOR A NEW ENVIRONMENT?

Martin Graham is Chief Executive of the Norfolk and Suffolk Probation Trust and takes the lead for the Probation Chiefs' Association nationally on courts and sentencing issues. Educated at Trinity Hall, Cambridge and Manchester University he began as a probation officer in the West Midlands, at Bilston near Wolverhampton, before progressing to senior positions at Walsall and in Norfolk where, before taking up his present post, he rose to become Chief Probation Officer for the Norfolk Probation area under the National Probation Service.

PROBATION AND THE MAGISTRACY:
A NEW RELATIONSHIP FOR A NEW ENVIRONMENT?

Martin Graham

Historical Context

Just over 100 years ago, the Probation of Offenders Act 1907 put on a statutory footing the appointment by magistrates of probation officers to work in local courts, thus formalising an arrangement which had existed informally since the latter part of the 19th century. The police court missioners had developed a role within the courts for taking into their care those defendants who were 'lost' but 'redeemable'. That redemption would include helping them to find jobs, to get off the drink, in short to become respectable citizens. This process had become known as 'probation', meaning proving, testing, giving someone a second chance.

Over the century or more since then there has always been a close and interdependent relationship between the magistracy and the probation service. Despite the many changes which probation has faced, moving from its historical role to 'advise, assist and befriend' its 'clients' through to being re-defined as an enforcement agency and more recently implementing a national model of 'offender management'. Magistrates have continued to look to the probation service for assessments of defendants which will assist the court to pass the most appropriate sentence in individual cases. Specifically, magistrates want to know what type of intervention might have the best prospect of preventing further offending by addressing the root causes of the defendant's offending behaviour whilst probation staff want to know what magistrates are expecting them to deliver when they have passed a community sentence.

Magistrates and the Governance of the Probation Service

For many years, probation committees were directly involved in the appointment of probation officers. Comprised largely of magistrates, these committees provided the governance for their local probation service. In 2001, however, the National Probation Service was established, with the previous 54 probation committees reducing to 42 probation areas co-terminous with police force areas. The governance for each probation area was now to be provided by a probation board which included fewer magistrates than the previous probation committees, drawing instead on appointed board members with a variety of skills and experience, some of whom happened to be magistrates. For some probation areas, this led to a significant diminution of magistrates' involvement in their local governance with a consequent loss of sentencing expertise and perspective.

This new national structure, which was overseen by the National Probation Directorate, lasted less than a decade. The Carter Report published in January 2004[1] paved the way for the establishment of the National Offender Management Service (NOMS) which brought together the probation and prison services under one organization, initially within the Home Office but since 2003 within the Ministry of Justice. The Carter Report also floated the idea of 'contestability', i.e. the breaking up the monopoly of provision which the probation and prison services had historically enjoyed by creating a competitive market place open to a range of other providers in the private and third sectors for the delivery of services to offenders.

In order to prepare the probation service for this new competitive environment and to enable it to better survive in an increasingly harsh economic climate, the 42 probation areas were replaced, with effect from April 2010, by 35 probation trusts, five voluntary mergers involving 12 probation areas having taken place as part of the trust application process. Trust status was expected to deliver a range of freedoms and flexibilities which would enable probation trusts to operate more like businesses. In reality very few of these have yet been delivered and although probation trusts are designated as non-departmental public bodies operating under a contractual relationship with the Secretary of State, there remain many areas in which trusts are subject to central control, not least in respect of functions such as IT, estates and facilities.

The governance arrangements for the new probation trusts moved to trust boards. Under a ruling from the Senior Presiding Judge in July 2010, magistrates were specifically excluded from being formal members of probation trust boards because it was felt that there would be a conflict of interest between their judicial function and independence and a competitive environment within which a probation trust might potentially be bidding to retain its own work. This prohibition was amended in 2011 to allow the following:

- magistrates who sit exclusively in the family proceedings courts can hold formal membership of a trust board;

- magistrates can also sit on a trust board outside their local justice area, but only in a private capacity, i.e. not representing the judiciary; and

- magistrates may sit on a trust board in a non-voting, observer or adviser capacity.[2]

Despite these concessions, the reality is that magistrates are now further removed from the governance of the probation service than at any point in the last 100 years.

Liaison Arrangements between Magistrates and the Probation Service

As magistrates have become less and less involved in the governance of the probation service, effective liaison between sentencers and local probation staff has been ever more crucial. Historically, probation case committees were the arenas where probation officers reported back to magistrates on the work they were doing with the offenders who had been put under their supervision and it was those committees which made decisions about whether revocation for good progress might be appropriate in individual cases. Case committees subsequently gave way to probation liaison committees which, rather than being concerned with individual cases, were a forum for the probation service to inform magistrates more generally about the work they were undertaking with those who were 'on probation'.

In recent years the Senior Presiding Judge has issued guidance on the liaison arrangements between the judiciary, including magistrates, and the probation service. These have resulted in a more businesslike approach to liaison with those passing sentence accompanied by an expectation that probation areas would provide more performance data to sentencers as well as information about the availability and effectiveness of a range of interventions being delivered within local bench areas. This guidance was updated and re-issued in December 2011 as already noted above.

Alongside the development of more effective liaison arrangements, many probation trusts have also sought ways of engaging with magistrates through key training events, particularly around new legislation such as Criminal Justice Acts, as with that in 2003. At its best this has resulted in stronger working relationships between magistrates and probation and a growing confidence in both the advice being given in the court context and the material being provided at liaison events about services being delivered to offenders. These arrangements have generally worked well and probation trusts and Her Majesty's Courts and Tribunal Service (HMCTS) have sought innovative ways of ensuring that magistrates are kept up-to-date through a range of media.

The Future of the Relationship Between the Magistracy and Probation

In recent years the effective liaison arrangements described above have started to come under strain due to resource pressures, primarily on HMCTS but also to a lesser extent on probation trusts. A snapshot survey of the 35 probation trusts carried out in 2011 found that, of the 27 trusts which responded, all had managed to maintain the resources they were putting into liaison with sentencers and in a small number of trusts this resource had actually been increased. However, 11 (41%) had experienced a reduction in magistrates' engagement with liaison activity in the previous 12 months whilst the other 16 were anticipating such a reduction in 2012 and beyond. This was particularly noticeable in some, but not all, larger rural areas, where magistrates often have to make significant journeys to attend liaison events. This is likely to be exacerbated as pressure on budgets grows year-on-year.

So, can or should magistrates and probation recover the relationship that they once had?

At the time of writing this chapter, the Ministry of Justice had just published two major consultation documents, 'Punishment and Reform: Effective Community Sentences' and 'Punishment and Reform: Effective Probation Services'.[3] The former, when translated into law, will, as with previous criminal justice legislation, require magistrates and probation to work closely together to ensure effective implementation. The latter, with its recommendations for the creation of a pure purchaser/provider split in probation, will potentially reserve to a public sector probation trust responsibility for delivering court services, the offender management of high risk cases and public interest decisions in respect of lower risk offenders (e.g. initial risk assessment, breach, etc.) and the commissioning of other providers to deliver all interventions and the general offender management of lower risk cases.

If such a fundamental change in the structure of the probation service takes place with the development of a competitive market place for services to offenders, then it is difficult to envisage any return to the involvement of magistrates in the governance of probation. It is therefore of increasing importance that the liaison arrangements between magistrates and probation are strengthened. The best of the current arrangements need to become the norm, but in particular probation must be able to reach all magistrates, not just those who already have an interest in probation. Whether this is achievable in an era of reducing resources with magistrates who are, after all, volunteers, is debatable. It has proved near impossible even in times of plenty for probation to access all magistrates, so it seems unlikely that this will happen in the current political and financial environment.

However, if the Government's intentions are to be realised in relation to the increased use of community sentences, the delivery of probation services by a variety of providers and a reduction in re-offending rates for offenders being managed in the community, then finding ways to deliver effective liaison between probation and all magistrates has never been more important.

Endnotes

1. Carter, P (2003), *Managing Offenders, Reducing Crime: A New Approach*, London: Ministry of Justice.

2. 'Judicial Membership of Probation Trusts: Guidance issued by The Rt. Hon. Lord Justice Goldring, Senior Presiding Judge', December 2010.

3. *Punishment and Reform: Effective Probation Services* (2012), Consultation Paper CP7/2012, London: Ministry of Justice; and *Punishment and Reform: Effective Community Sentences* (2012), Consultation Paper CP8/2012, London: Ministry of Justice.

7

AT THE CROSSROADS, BUT WHICH WAY TO GO?

Barry Godfrey is Professor of Social Justice at Liverpool University. He has 20 years of experience in researching comparative criminology, particularly international crime history, desistence studies and longitudinal studies of offending. He has published a number of books, most recently Godfrey, Cox, and Farrall (2010), *Serious Offenders*; Godfrey, Lawrence, and Williams (2007), *History and Crime*; and Godfrey, Cox, and Farrall (2007), *Criminal Lives: Family, Employment and Offending*. He has been a magistrate in the South Cheshire courts since 1998.

AT THE CROSSROADS, BUT WHICH WAY TO GO?

Barry Godfrey

Until the eighteenth century, criminals who had been hanged on the gallows, and people who had committed suicide, were often buried at the crossroads of major junctions. It may be something of a myth, but legend has it that the tortured souls of the damned would be confused by the choice of direction, and finding their way back to their tormentors would be made more difficult. Which way to go? The modern magistrate could be forgiven for feeling similarly confused. Should the magistracy take the road towards professionalisation (of magistrates themselves through increased and enhanced training, or by introducing more and more salaried professional sentencers into the system?) Are we pulled towards public satisfaction indexes; having to bolster public confidence in the criminal justice system through 'magistrates in the community' and 650th anniversary events? Proving our usefulness by taking on more serious offences such as domestic burglaries in order to save public finances? All of these routes? Or none, just drifting out of business as so many have predicted over the last century or so? Indeed, Lord Merthyr commented to the 1948 Royal Commission that

> I think it is merely a matter of time before lay justices disappear. It is a question not of whether but when they should be replaced.[1]

What would the criminal justice system, or indeed society, look like without the lay magistracy? The magistrates have continued to deal with the vast bulk of judicial business ever since minor offending was removed from the higher courts, which were expensive and irregularly-held, to the more convenient magistrates' courts in the mid-to-late-nineteenth century. In 1857, when criminal statistics were first annually recorded and published, just over half a million defendants were proceeded against in magistrates' courts. In the 1870s and 1880s the figures were virtually unchanged. On the eve of the First World War, the number had risen to 690,000 and by the start of World War II the number of defendants appearing before local summary courts was 760,000. Now the magistrates keep around 95 per cent of all defendants proceeded against within their courts, dealing with almost three million defendants in 2011 (approximately 100 defendants per magistrate per year if we want to quantify justice in that way). If one considers that many defendants are multiply charged, then this is a huge amount of cases which are being dealt with in the magistrates' courts.

So the first effect would be a huge hole in judicial capacity which, despite the wildest of blue skies thinking, could not be filled by professional colleagues. Could the private sector step in to plug the gap? Both Labour and Conservative governments have drawn the private sector into traditional public sectors activities, so it would not be unreasonable to think that the increasing marketisation of justice could ensue in the twenty-first century. We could envisage a system where victims of criminal damage, shoplifting and minor assaults were dealt with by a pay-for-justice system, similar to a small claims court, where only financial penalties (enforceable in civil courts if unpaid) were distributed. This would actually return us to a pre-nineteenth century model of justice where dispute-resolution took primacy over 'criming' acts of harm. It would fail for the same reasons that the system was changed in the nineteenth-century—the system would lack legitimacy; and, one imagines, also fail to capture and retain the confidence of the public (although it was cheaper and easier).

A system which appeals more to policy-makers than victims would see an extension of police-issued penalty notices in respect of more serious offences (even now they cover many offences which the public might judge as serious if the system was more widely known and understood). Out-of-court disposals are running at about half a million a year, in addition to the quarter of a million police cautions, and the 130,000 penalty notices for disorder (PNDs) which are issued each year. Together these have reduced the load on the courts to more manageable proportions by taking offences which, in reality, are not complex sentencing matters, nor do they require a view to be taken on the offender's criminal career. Road traffic offences often involve mandatory sentences (periods of disqualification, points for speeding, and so on), and automatic dispensations of fines through the post are more convenient than attending a local court (and courts are becoming less local as closure programmes bite). However, for anything other than very minor offending, it is unlikely that the public would accept the legitimacy of the system, or that it would tackle criminal careers. One of the main but little articulated claims of the magistracy has been that it saves money and future victims of crime by taking in the context of the offender's life as well as of the offence itself and appropriately sentencing offenders so that their criminal career is, if not stopped, then shortened.

The hacking away of the lay benches would also seem to attack a system of participatory democracy that is cherished in the UK. Across the political spectrum from green activists, through trade unionists, to a Conservative Prime Minister, there are calls for public duty and volunteerism to be extended, not reduced. The lay magistracy involves some 26,000 thousand people who regularly participate in public life, making a contribution to polity without being 'political'. It would seem perverse, therefore, to reduce public involvement when other initiatives are introduced to try to lever the public voice into power structures (the vaunted police and crime commissioners for example).

The alternatives to a fully-functioning hard-working lay magistracy seem beset by problems. So why contemplate the loss of our role at all? Surely the only route for magistrates at the crossroads is towards the sunny uplands? It seems not. Most magistrates are appointed with the impression that they are joining a viable, long-established, traditional and valued institution. However, within months of joining most probably, they will also have been told that 'things are changing' or are 'about to change'. Over the last 30 years or so, there has been an almost permanent revolution in, for example, court design (especially in youth courts), changes in procedures designed to speed up the administration of justice (from Narey Courts, to recent entreaties to 'Stop Delaying Justice!'[2]) and in levels of sentencing (in both the youth and adult courts). In the last decade however, we have been expecting game-changing shifts which could significantly affect the way that justice will be delivered in the UK. Fundamental changes have been mooted, and are already happening. Courts are closing because the physical estate is proving expensive to maintain in the new age of austerity. Recent reports and investigations discuss the merits of a professional bench over the lay magistracy.[3]

The Magistrates Association has been extremely active in refuting spurious challenges to the lay principle, but there is little by way of public outcry at the threat to the magistracy. This does not mean that there isn't an appreciation of the work carried out by the unpaid workhorses of the system, there may be a deep well of affection that could be drawn upon if the crunch comes, but it may be difficult to mobilise support in the media or amongst the general public.

So, how can the magistracy adapt and reinforce the contribution it makes to society? If it struggles to explain its usefulness to the general public at times, there should be an effort to reconnect with local communities. Embeddeness in local structures, physical as well as administrative, can be achieved. Magistrates can share facilities with civic centres, libraries, leisure centres even, to share and reduce costs. Courts would be placed alongside local authority bodies, medical practices, and educational facilities, as community assets. So long as the information highway connects the courts to the data they need (maybe directly from centralised systems) then the courts could be re-embedded into the locality in a way which reverses the current policy direction. The trick will be to retain the majesty of the law within everyday surroundings in order that the administration of justice retains its traditional legitimacy and authority. The critical test of the magistracy in the twenty-first century will be whether it delivers a system of justice which is accepted by local people (including victims and defendants) as well as policy-makers.

However, whichever path the magistracy takes at the crossroads, it is likely to be a bumpy one, but we should not fool ourselves that the way has ever been smooth. We have a robust system of justice, and we should have the confidence to find a way forward.

Endnotes

1. Quoted in Thomas Skyrme, *History of the Justices of the Peace* (1994), Chichester: Barry Rose, p.30. See also *Royal Commission on Justices of the Peace, Report Presented to Parliament by Command of His Majesty 1946-48*, Cmd. 7463, chaired by Lord DuParcq.

2. The term 'Narey Courts' is a reference to a 1999 initiative to speed up the business of magistrates' courts, led by Martin Narey. For 'Stop Delaying Justice!', see See http://www.crimeline.info/stop-delaying-justice/

3. Morgan R and Russell N (2000), *The Judiciary in the Magistrates Courts*, London: Home Office; Auld, Sir Robin (2001), *A Review of the Criminal Courts of England and Wales*, London: The Stationery Office; and *The Strengths and Skills of the Judiciary in Magistrates Courts* (2011), Ipsos MORI, Report, 9/11, London: Ministry of Justice.

8

WHERE NEXT FOR THE MAGISTRACY?

Roger Graef OBE is an award winning film-maker, criminologist, and writer best known for his unstaged observational films in normally closed places like government ministries, board rooms, prisons, special schools and probation or social work settings.

Many of his films have influenced policing and criminal justice policy. Most recently, The *Trouble with Adoption*: *A Panorama Special* helped the government promise of speedier adoptions, and encouraged thousands to offer to adopt children. His BBC1 series with Nick Ross, *The Truth About Crime*, measured for the first time how much crime and harm happened in one place over a fortnight. The handling of rape victims was changed by *An Allegation of Rape* in his ground-breaking series *Police*. He has made some 50 films on policing in ten different forces, on such themes as race, and the handling by multi-agency protection panel arrangements (MAPPAs) with regard to sex offenders. *In Search of Law and Order* influenced the Youth Justice Board's experimental work in juvenile justice.

Roger Graef writes and broadcasts regularly on criminal justice. He is the author of *Talking Blues, Police in their Own Words, Living Dangerously; Young Offenders in Their Own Words*; and *Why Restorative Justice?* In 2004, he was the first documentary maker to be awarded the BAFTA Fellowship for lifetime achievement and in 2006 was given an OBE. He was a Visiting Professor at Oxford University, and is now Visiting Professor at the Mannheim Centre for Criminology at the London School of Economics. He has been an independent adviser to the Metropolitan Police on race since 1999, and is an adviser to the Sentencing Council.

WHERE NEXT FOR THE MAGISTRACY?

Roger Graef

The magistracy is indeed at a crossroads. But the way ahead is shrouded in cloud. The only clear direction heads towards a dead end. It comes from the recent closure of magistrates' courts and the expansion of district judges. It is 'sending a message'—as ministers like to call longer sentences—loudly and all too clearly that magistrates are less important than they have been and are heading for extinction. Worse still, local justice is being trumped by 'efficiency', consistency and cost savings. So much for the Big Society, of which the magistracy is a long term and distinguished example.

Whatever lip service is paid to keeping the magistracy alive, this strikes at the heart of its *raison d'etre*. The very point of the magistracy is that justice is administered to the community by the community—or rather by respected members of it to those accused of forfeiting that respect. The notion is that such a communitarian relationship will lead those who have strayed to mend their ways. And those wrongly accused will have their innocence more easily recognised by their near neighbours. Even if most of them were toffs, it was presumed they would have more sympathy and understanding of local conditions and motivations than more remote bewigged judges.

This echoes the Cree Indians' optimistic view of the role of the justice system—to close the circle broken by crime. But the increasing obsession with efficiency and punishment as crime control with the vast expansion of new criminal offences, has in reality undermined the communitarian rhetoric of successive governments. In its attempt to make the criminal justice syetem (CJS) more of a system, it loses the distinctive personality that local magistrates in truly local courts can bring.

This contradiction is being lived daily by offenders, victims, and above all sentencers, especially magistrates. They are expected to use their sentences to punish past behaviour, deter future repetition by the accused and others, help them back to the straight and narrow, and, in doing all this, promote community safety. All commendable goals. But as David Faulkner and Ros Burnett argue In their important book, *Where Next For Criminal Justice?*,[1] there is no guidance for sentencers about how to weight these principles when they conflict

The absurdly long sentences for rioters convicted of first offences and minor thefts are prime examples of system failure. Proportionality and common sense went out the window. The courts, whatever respect they may have won in the media and among politicians, lost it in the eyes of many offenders, who have been unnecessarily criminalised, and their families, who have been unfairly stigmatised. And their spell in a place which the Home Office have said 'can be an expensive way of making bad people worse'[2] has only increased the likelihood of their reoffending when they come out of prison.

Despite being unpaid, and increasingly marginalised, many magistrates take their role very seriously. It is a noble, dignified act to give up so much time unpaid, to help your fellow local citizens to go straight, or avoid unfair punishment.

At best, magistrates recognise the causes of crime, and try to use their increasingly limited means to address them. At worst, they can seem distant and high handed, as with the famous Bow Street magistrate dealing with a vagrant begging in front of the Royal Opera House:

> 'You're a frightful nuisance to respectable opera-goers...Why do you do it?'

'No money, guv,' came the answer.

'Rubbish! Fined ten pounds! Next case.'

The wider membership of the bench in terms of gender, class and ethnic background has somewhat narrowed the social and experiential distance between the bench and those who appear in front of it. But that gap is in serious danger of widening again as unemployment rises, as does property crime from extended periods of austerity, benefit cuts, and unemployment,

So where next for the magistracy under such uncomfortable circumstances?

Of the choices laid out by David Faulkner in his introduction, I would encourage magistrates to become involved in criminal justice services like community justice panels, problem-solving courts, probation, prisons and rehabilitation. The more they can see offenders as human beings like their own friends and family, with similar goals and values, the more they will use carrots rather than sticks to help them change.

There is some risk of justices of the peace becoming too involved to make objective assessments of appropriate disposals. But the notion of detached largely punitive justice administered *de haut en bas,* aloof from and indifferent to the circumstances of the crime and the criminal themselves flies in the face of what we know speaks to offenders' consciences, and affects the likelihood of their re-offending.

Despite its appeal to politicians and the media, punishment alone is not working. The reconviction rate for convicted offenders sent to prison is shamingly high. But given the far greater number of undetected offences, the failure of sentencing and prisons to stop crime is glaringly obvious. That certain categories of volume crime have fallen regularly is more to do with target hardening and other crime prevention measures than deterrent sentences. Indeed, custody increases the chance of re-offending by a geometric proportion. If deterrence worked, prisons would be empty of recidivists rather than full of them. Punitive sentences are especially inadequate with persistent offenders. They have been punished often arbitrarily from an early age.[3] The threat of more merely feeds their sense of Us Against Them. And it reduces the likelihood of being reintegrated into society.

Community justice panels are part of a spectrum of restorative justice options based on the principle of 'reintegrative shaming'. The power of those two words when used together is hard to exaggerate. Unlike normal courts and sentences, treated as a game by many young offenders, and an occupational hazard by older ones, restorative justice options address parts of offenders' decision-making the normal justice system leaves out.

Focusing on who did what and when and to whom leaves out why, and what could be done to stop it happening again. It also leaves the victim on the sidelines — despite the rhetoric of the now departed Labour Government to rebalance the system in their favour.

Professional judges largely prefer process-based sentencing, dealing efficiently (sic!) with the huge number of criminal offences and sentencing guidelines that limit their choices. Try as they might, it is assembly line justice. Even the good ones lament that they seldom find out about the impact of their sentences.

Community justice panels and problem-solving courts have the opposite goal — not just dealing with as many cases as possible in the minimum time necessary, but exploring the causes of the crimes, and the local options to address them. I have sat in the Red Hook Court in Brooklyn, and seen the judge demand to visit the housing of a defaulting tenant who complained about non-repairs to his ceiling and plumbing. He doubted the housing department's insistence that they had done what was needed, and that the tenant simply deserved punishment for his arrears. The court was near the house, so the judge adjourned, went to the flat and saw that the tenant was right. It was the housing department that was chastised. Justice was done and seen to be done. The tenant, his family, neighbours and friends, all had their view of the court enhanced. Watching such a compassionate and effective judge in action on the level of cases dealt with in magistrates' courts here was not only inspiring, it made me impatient with the failure to spread the model from the court in North Liverpool on the grounds it has yet to prove worth such costs as are attached to it.

The culture of local involvement cannot be installed from Whitehall. It needs to grow organically. It needs to build on local champions' willingness to use it, and on examples which become part of local knowledge. This takes time, and is an iterative process. It also takes local credibility.

By closing so many magistrates' courts, the Ministry of Justice has torn up those precious local connections, or at least stretched them to breaking point. My prescription for reviving the magistracy is to rebuild local involvement in whatever ways are feasible and deemed appropriate. Sitting on community justice panels — less elaborate than problem-solving courts and using more local people — is one such way. The experience of such panels in America in states like Vermont is that they transform the purely punitive process into rebuilding lives as well as repairing the damage caused by the offence, and winning the respect of local citizens previously sceptical or downright hostile to any contact with offenders.

Specialist courts for domestic violence, like the children and families court in Westminster, at which lawyers only appear for the local authority, create an informal and direct connection between the bench and in that court, parents trying to recover custody of their children by reassuring the court — or rather specifically the district judge Nicholas Crichton whom they know and trust — that they have given up drink or drugs. He is tough but tender, firm but fair — clearly interested in their progress, but clear about his concerns about sustained abstinence, and the consequences of backsliding. Such personal involvement is not a disadvantage to the goals of sentencing — greater community safety, improving the chances of desistence, encouraging offenders to take more responsibility for their actions. It increases them dramatically. Surely an end devoutly to be wished.

Moreover, the long term price of cost savings and efficiency drives that cut the Gordian Knot between local magistrates' courts and their communities will be far, far higher in social costs, lost taxes, and prison and mental hospital places. That I write this when prisons are at an all time high, while support systems are being cut dramatically, merely proves the point painfully, and expensively. Having informed and respected citizens see this for themselves when also making decisions about offenders' futures can only strengthen their judgement.

Endnotes

---

1. Faulkner D and Burnett R (2012), *Where Next for Criminal Justice?*, Bristol: Policy Press.

2. Home Office (1990), *Crime, Justice and Protecting the Public*, Cm 965, 6, London: HMSO.

3. Farrington, D and West, D (1993), 'Criminal and Penal Life Histories of Chronic Offenders: Risk and Protective Factors and Early Identification', *Criminal Behaviour and Mental Health*, 3, 492-523.

9

DIFFICULT TIMES AHEAD?

Kate Green was elected MP for Stretford and Urmston in May 2010. She is currently shadow spokesperson for Women and Equality. Prior to her election she was Chief Executive of the Child Poverty Action Group, and before that Director of the National Council for One Parent Families (now Gingerbread). She is a longstanding campaigner against poverty and inequality, and was a member of the National Employment Panel which advised ministers on labour market policies, and Chair of the London Child Poverty Commission, reporting to the Mayor of London and local councillors. She is a member of the Greater Manchester Poverty Commission and now chairs the All-party Parliamentary Group on Poverty.

Kate Green also served as a magistrate for 16 years, and takes a particular interest in the experiences of women in the penal system, and how best to rehabilitate them to prevent future reoffending.

DIFFICULT TIMES AHEAD?

Kate Green

These are difficult times for our society. Economic uncertainty and social instability go hand-in-hand. The rise in crime that typically accompanies economic austerity is well documented, and the signs are showing: personal crime rose by eleven per cent last year, after falling over the previous decade by 40 per cent. Very worryingly, an increase in domestic violence often accompanies economic downturn, exacerbated because victims are often prevented financially from fleeing abuse. Our society feels more fragile — while the causes of last summer's riots are complex, a local police commander told me of his certainty that we will see such incidents again. Radical protest, often motivated by austerity policies (and by no means all of it criminal or violent), has returned to our streets, while so-called hate crime, political extremism, and the threat of terror, both homegrown and external, worry away at the back of our minds.

Modern-day pressures — debt, worklessness, homelessness, social tension — hardly come as new to the lay magistracy. In their 650-year history, magistrates have seen all this before. And society too will prove itself resilient, with people adapting, and supporting one another through tough times.

Nonetheless, we face a challenging context in which the lay judiciary must do its work. Magistrates are all too aware from their courtroom experience of the nature of the pressures faced in modern-day life. They see, day in, day out, the young people left without the chance of a job, caught up in a world of petty crime. They see the sofa surfing, the constant moving-on faced by the homeless, with all the difficulty of sustaining stable personal relationships with friends and family, or forming an identity with the community. They see the antisocial behaviour that results from having no real stake in society. They see the narrative of irresponsible greed at the top reflected in the sense of entitlement and aggrieved acquisitiveness of those with much less. They see those whom the system has failed to support—those leaving local authority care, those without basic skills or qualifications, those who've been round the criminal justice system again and again—and to little apparent effect.

This is not to imply that because they're poor, people will turn to crime. Nor is it to suggest that criminal behaviour is the preserve of the disadvantaged and marginalised. But tough times will have an impact on crime levels, and magistrates, who deal with the vast majority of cases in court, will see the social consequences, and the damaging effect on communities and individuals, whether as victims of or perpetrators of crime. It's of real concern therefore that the likely rise in workload for the magistracy that will result from adverse economic conditions could coincide with increased difficulty in recruiting and retaining magistrates, itself the result of a range of financial pressures.

First, with unemployment at record levels and rising, candidates for the magistracy may be increasingly reluctant to apply, while existing magistrates may feel pressure to step down, in order to keep scarce jobs. Pressure to bear down on magistrates' expenses will make the situation worse, indeed untenable for some. Employers meanwhile may be less sympathetic to requests for time off for magistrates to fulfil their duties on the bench when businesses are under pressure, while government enthusiasm for removing perceived 'red tape' from business may send signals to employers that requests to work flexibly to undertake public duties can be turned aside. What's more, despite the government's proclaimed commitment to so-called localism, local justice is also under threat, with more courts closing in the drive for cost-cutting and greater efficiency in the criminal justice system. Yet the time and cost of travelling to a court further from home may deter potential applicants or drive existing magistrates from the bench.

The consequence for the magistracy could therefore be significant pressure on numbers, with people no longer able to afford to serve as magistrates. And that would be deeply worrying: it would have an inevitably adverse impact on quality, and create a major step backwards in terms of the diversity of the bench. Young people, women, the disabled, and those from minority ethnic communities, who already face the greatest economic and labour market disadvantage, would likely be the first to be shut out.

At the same time, moves to widen magistrates' powers, by increasing their sentencing capacity to a maximum custodial sentence of 12 months,[1] which have been welcomed by the Magistrates Association, will create demand for more and magistrates with greater experience to handle the more serious cases these sentences attract. More training of magistrates will be needed: again that requires magistrates to have the time to give.

So we may be heading to a perfect storm, of a rising and more demanding workload at the same time as the number of well-qualified magistrates available to deal with it comes under increasing pressure in various ways. That in turn heightens the risk of poorer quality decision-making, as fewer magistrates are pressed to make more decisions more quickly, threatening a crisis of credibility for the magistracy, and a collapse in public confidence.

The situation is serious, yet the cumulative effect of these different socio-economic pressures on the future of lay justice has been the subject of surprisingly little debate. The 650th anniversary must therefore be seized upon to drive a national conversation about the tensions, pressures and risks the magistracy faces. If local justice is important, how can it be cost-effectively sustained? If a diverse, representative magistracy matters for the credibility and legitimacy of our justice system, how can that diversity be protected, and the risk of losing good magistrates because they can't afford to serve, be properly addressed? What modelling has been done of future trends in crime, and of the impact of changes to sentencing powers, and is the magistracy adequately resourced to deal with them? How do we ensure that proper attention is given to the widest possible understanding of the causes and drivers of crime, and to ensuring the right social policies, including but not exclusively sentencing policies, are put in place to help to bring it down?

These are not easy questions in difficult times, but without satisfactory answers, the lay magistracy risks becoming the preserve of a privileged, narrowly-drawn group with the time and money to serve, or even no longer viable, adequately skilled, or seen as relevant. With 650 years of history to protect, we must therefore urgently embark on this vital debate.

Endnotes

1. This greater sentencing power for magistrates is already provided for in section 154 Criminal Justice Act 2003, but like much of the 2003 Act sentencing regime for magistrates' courts that provision has never been brought into force.

10

'TWAS EVER THUS

Heather Hallett was educated at Brockenhurst Grammar School in the New Forest and St Hugh's College, Oxford. She was called to the Bar in 1972. In 1989 she became a QC and was appointed a Recorder of the Crown Court. She became a Bencher of Inner Temple in 1993 and Leader of the South Eastern Circuit a year later. She was the first woman to become Chairman of the Bar Council in 1998. She became a full-time judge of the High Court in 1999 and was promoted to the Court of Appeal in 2005. She was the Treasurer of the Inner Temple for 2011.

Lady Justice Hallett was appointed as a member and latterly Vice-Chairman of the Judicial Appointments Commission. She is currently Chairman of the Judicial College and Vice-President of the Queen's Bench Division. She acted as Coroner at the inquest into the deaths of the 52 victims of the July 7th London bombings.

Heather Hallett is married to fellow lawyer, Nigel Wilkinson QC and has two sons. She divides her time between London and the coast. Her interests are music, theatre and games.

'TWAS EVER THUS

Heather Hallett

In 2011 I was Treasurer of the Inner Temple, one of the four Inns of Court, institutions which have served the system of justice with distinction since the fourteenth century. It seemed to me only fitting, therefore, that the Inner Temple should host a celebration of the 650th anniversary of another proud institution: the magistracy. Arguably, we were a little late in our celebrations given that in 1195, Richard 1 commissioned 'keepers of the peace', to preserve the country's peace in unruly areas and an Act of 1327 referred to 'good and lawful men' to be appointed in every county in the land to 'guard the peace'. However, it was not until 1361 that the title of justice of the peace was first created and we were, therefore, justified in celebrating its 650th anniversary in 2011.

Few institutions can boast such a long history. Why has the magistracy survived so long? It is not without its critics. Throughout my time at the Bar and on the Bench there have been repeated new policy initiatives which have led some magistrates to fear that their very existence was under threat. Yet, in 2012 the institution thrives with upwards of 26,000 members.

To my mind there can be only one reason for this: as an institution the magistracy has proved its worth. It deserves to survive. The survival of the magistracy has depended upon the recognition of three essential principles enshrined in the Act of 1361:

1. The 'preservation of the sovereign's peace' is vital to a stable and strong society;

2. Ordinary citizens should play a significant role in deciding the guilt or innocence of an accused and in the punishment of the guilty; and

3. Justice should be delivered at a local level where at all possible.

I should emphasise that I use the adjective 'ordinary' to distinguish the lay from the professional judge — many magistrates are far from ordinary!

Ordinary citizens appointed from among the communities they serve are well-equipped to ensure the preservation of the sovereign's peace in those communities. They understand local conditions and pressures in a way that a professionally qualified judge sitting in judgment miles away from his or her own area may struggle to do. They bring to their role a wealth of experience and breadth of knowledge not only of their communities, but of the world outside the law. The abiding strength of the magistracy is that it is comprised of local citizens and is extremely diverse in its membership in terms of gender, ethnicity and range of backgrounds. Its understanding of local communities is a basic principle in community justice and it is the embodiment of the so called Big Society.

The very fact that the magistracy still deals with over 95 per cent of all criminal matters brought to court and enjoys a wide-ranging civil jurisdiction including a significant contribution to the family courts is persuasive testament to its effectiveness. The rate of appeals against magistrates' decisions is minimal — about 0.5 per cent of some 1.38 million decisions made in any one year. The objective evidence would indicate that the quality of justice dispensed by magistrates is fair, proportionate and of a high quality. It comes as no surprise to me to learn, therefore, that the report into the judiciary in the magistrates' courts indicated that the magistracy is a cost effective and efficient way of dealing with the many minor crimes that come before the courts.[1]

The high standards are due in part to the selection process which ensures the selection of the best but also to the fact that magistrates are mentored, well trained and appraised on a regular basis. I know from my personal experience with the Judicial Studies Board (now Judicial College) that magistrates show enthusiasm and a high level of commitment to everything they undertake. They are skilled and knowledgeable participants in the planning and delivery of training programmes. They are willing to mentor new appointees and support longer serving colleagues through the appraisal system. Indeed, the magistracy has led the way in both mentoring and appraisal, the benefits of which are widely acknowledged and which many would now wish to see extended throughout the justice system to all professional judges.

The magistracy of the twentieth and twenty-first century has shown itself responsive to change. Some change has been essential (for example to achieve a greater degree of consistency in sentencing) and some change forced upon an unwilling bench (for example the closure of courthouses). Whatever their personal views, for the most part, magistrates simply knuckle down and do their best to embrace the change.

I shall focus on just three of those changes: an increase in the use of professional judges in the magistrates' courts, reduced workload and court closures.

District Judges and Magistrates

There may be a possible tension in the relationship between the district judges (magistrates' courts) and the magistrates, with some magistrates understandably concerned that the professional judge may take all the more complex and interesting work leaving them with a diet of road traffic offences and pleas of guilty. However, significant improvements have been made and will continue to be made in the relationship. Magistrates have now been brought fully within the judicial family and they take their rightful place alongside their professional colleagues on the Judges' Council, in deciding how best to advise the Lord Chief Justice on everything to do with the system of justice.

I am confident that with goodwill on both sides if any tension remains, it can be removed by proper dialogue, sensitive listing of cases, and creative listing. There are obvious cases for which a professional judge may be better suited, for example cases which last several days or which involve complex issues of law such as extradition. There are many other cases for which a lay bench is eminently suited. However, there are also occasions when mixed benches of magistrates and district judges are ideal. I would hope that when mixed panels are convened, both the district judges and the magistrates find the experience beneficial and learn from each other.

Reduced Workloads

Many (but not all) court centres have seen a reduction in workload. Some blame the rising use of administrative or out-of-court disposals, many of which have been used for serious offences such as assault occasioning actual bodily harm. If serious offences are seen to be dealt with in an inappropriately lenient manner it might well undermine confidence in the justice system. In this respect, the magistracy could usefully play a wider role in monitoring, ex post facto, the use of such disposals, thereby reassuring the public that independent judicial office holders protect their interests.

Court Closures

Reduced workloads and over-capacity in the courts estate has forced Her Majesty's Courts and Tribunal Service to close a number of courthouses. Many magistrates now have to travel relatively long distances to dispense their 'local justice' from a court centre in what they would consider another district. They fear a loss of their sense of identity and an inability to deliver justice locally to the community they were meant to serve. There are no easy answers. Everyone has to make sacrifices in times of recession. I fear this is one of those changes where magistrates must simply knuckle down and make the best of what they may consider to be a bad job. Local justice may not be quite as local as it once was in some areas, but it is still relatively local. The challenge for the magistracy is to ensure that, wherever magistrates sit, they continue to serve the community they were appointed to serve.

Plainly, the courts must change and procedures must be streamlined. We must all play our part in improving the quality of the delivery of 'justice' and make the trial process as smooth as possible. The magistracy has embraced and must continue to embrace new ideas to that end. It engaged actively in the Criminal Justice: Simple, Speedy Summary (CJSSS) initiative to improve case management and in the 2012 video entitled 'Stop Delaying Justice' designed to reduce unnecessary adjournments.

Should the trial process end in conviction there comes the knotty problem of sentencing, an area which has become increasingly complex over the years. The role of the magistrates has here evolved. The advent of community and problem-solving courts has shifted the emphasis from punishment to an understanding of why offending behaviour is exhibited. The experience of the drug and problem-solving courts indicates that offenders react positively when an authority figure such as a magistrate shows an interest in how they are progressing on a sentence. Many offenders begin the process of rehabilitation more quickly than would otherwise be the case. For every offender deterred from a long and costly criminal career, the benefits to society are obvious. Thus, the magistracy has made and continues to make a significant contribution to the public's confidence in the justice system.

If asked whether the magistracy is at a crossroads, my answer would be: 'Yes, but 'twas ever thus'. There is a clear and definitive direction for it to travel: straight ahead. I have no doubt the magistracy has the commitment to face any challenges head on and it will do so with the same vigour and dedication it has shown over 650 years. The principle of the ordinary citizen engaging in the justice system is as solid today as it was back in 1361. It would be a brave man and woman who tried to say otherwise.

Endnote

1. Ministry of Justice (2011), *The Strengths and Skills of the Judiciary in the Magistrates' Courts,* Ministry of Justice Research Series, 9/11, London: Ministry of Justice.

11

HISTORICAL PERSPECTIVE

John Hostettler was a practising solicitor in London for 35 years as well as undertaking political and civil liberties cases in Nigeria, Germany and Aden. He sat as a magistrate for a number of years and has also been a chairman of tribunals. He played a leading role in the abolition of flogging in British colonial prisons and served on a Home Office Committee to revise the rules governing electoral law in Britain. He holds a number of degrees and three doctorates and has written various books of which *Dissenters, Radicals, Heretics and Blasphemers: The Flame of Revolt that Shines through English History* (Waterside Press, 2012) is his 21st. His biographical works include those on social reformer Thomas Wakley and legal icons Sir James Fitzjames Stephen, Sir Edward Carson, Sir Edward Coke, Lord Halsbury and Sir Matthew Hale. Others encompass those on the jury, adversary trial, the abolition of capital punishment and the Rule of Law. In 2009, his book *Sir William Garrow: His Life, Times and Fight for Justice* (Waterside Press), co-written with Richard Braby (a descendant of William Garrow), rescued from obscurity the story of one of English law's forgotten reformers, as mirrored by the prime-time BBC TV series 'Garrow's Law'.

HISTORICAL PERSPECTIVE

John Hostettler

The lay magistracy in England has a long history going back to the Middle Ages. There were cautious beginnings in an effort to control the considerable violence during conflict between the powerful barons. Further, by the early fourteenth century the sheriffs, who were meant to dispense criminal justice had themselves grown over-mighty and corrupt. In order to circumvent them and deal with the violence King Edward III created a new commission made up of local gentry who were charged with keeping the peace. At first they only held prisoners in custody until they could bring them before the itinerant royal justices who delivered the gaols. But by 1344 they had acquired the authority to try and punish prisoners and by the Statute of Westminster (1361)[1] they became officially justices of the peace as they remain today.

The first paragraph of the 1361 Act reads:

> FIRST, That in every County of England shall be assigned for the keeping of the Peace, one Lord, and with him three or four of the most worthy in the County, with some learned in the law, and they shall have Power to restrain the Offenders, Rioters and all other Barators, and to pursue, arrest, take, and chastise them according to their trespass or offence.

Other paragraphs added extended powers and at first the justices were paid a small sum but this later lapsed and, of course, the number of justices increased substantially in the following centuries.

Independence

In their early days, the justices were the administrative, legal and political deputies of the Crown in the counties. Indeed, they became the effective rulers of the counties to such an extent that in the seventeenth century Coke could say of their rule, 'It is such a form of subordinate government for the tranquillity and quiet of the realm, as no part of the Christian world hath the like'.[2] That continued throughout their history and the justices of the peace have provided an efficient system of local government and administration of justice. At times they have come under severe censure, as with the 'trading justices' of London implicated in corruption and dealings over stolen goods in the eighteenth century. Such censure was often justified by modern standards.

Nevertheless, historically magistrates were famous for their degree of independence and they have often played an important role in times of crisis. As two legal writers have said:

> Their first concern was with the command structure of social control, over outbursts of rioting as well as day-to-day crime. They were the representatives of civil power when armed force was called in, the supervisors of police, the main prosecuting authorities, and often enough the judges.[3]

Historically, the administrative (until 1835) and judicial powers of the magistracy have been the foundation of criminal law and practice, generally at an undocumented and unlettered level, although in 1820 Chief Justice Abbott eulogised the magistracy, saying that the country was under a great obligation to justices of the peace.[4]

Expansion of Judicial Work

Then the year 1855 saw the enactment of a Criminal Justice Act[5] that paved the way for a huge expansion of the public judicial work of justices during the nineteenth and twentieth centuries which eventually led to their disposal of at least 94 per cent of all prosecutions in England and Wales. Earlier appointment to the bench was open only to those with wealth but that gradually changed and today magistrates are often teachers, manual workers and men and women from ethnic communities. As a consequence, today, the lay magistracy involves the people's participation as empowered citizens. Generally speaking it has the confidence of the public as a form of local democracy.

From the early days until the present time there have been many changes to the system and change today should not be dismissed out of hand. The law and legal institutions cannot remain static. The question is 'What kind of change is required?' The Auld Report[6] clearly, but incorrectly, expressed the view that the jury had largely outlived its usefulness so governments of both colour attempt to weaken the lay magistracy and replace it with professionals. As a solicitor I have been involved in cases dealt with by district judges who have exhibited the high calibre required for the complicated cases before them. That they are needed is not in doubt. But their numbers are quietly and frequently being augmented and they should not be allowed to swamp the lay magistrates who are correctly seen as part of the same community as those who appear before them and part of our participatory democracy.

Bastion Against Oppression

As mentioned above, lay magistrates hear some 94 per cent or more of all criminal cases. This involvement of ordinary citizens in the administration of the law is a very old tradition and it is deeply rooted in our psyche. It is an integral part of the English and Welsh heritage. The function of magistrates is to decide cases on their merits acting as independent judges of fact and, with advice from their clerk, of law. As ordinary citizens, like the jury, they are a bastion against oppression, short cuts and mechanistic justice. Frequently, it is suggested that, although unpaid, magistrates are too expensive because their cases take longer than those of district judges. Further, they are no longer capable of dealing with the increased volume and complexity of the cases before them. The alternative put forward is for more full-time, paid and legally qualified district judges to establish a professional judiciary for all courts.

The late Sir Thomas Skyrme served the magistracy for many years as secretary of commissions for England and Wales and in 1991 he expressed the opinion that the work of magistrates was becoming so complex and wide-ranging that it perplexed even the lawyer magistrates. He argued, therefore, that some sort of reduction in the scope of the justices' duties was essential in the interests of efficiency.[7] Indeed, that has happened with licensing, probation, prisons and other functions. So efficiency replaces democratic participation in those functions and duties.

Lay magistrates receive intensive training and guidance which is undoubtedly necessary. But it can have the effect of reducing their independent role if they consider that they must make decisions on the basis of what they have been told. In my time on the bench I saw some magistrates direct their minds to the penalty to be imposed on the defendant before and rather than considering whether he or she might be innocent of the charge. Steps should be taken in magistrates' training to reinforce their understanding that they must decide independently on the basis of what they believe is right on the evidence they have heard.

A New Role

Magistrates are rightly proud of their history and the role the magistracy has played in the good governance of the country. But what is needed today is a magistracy with a new and more dynamic role. Justices need to be less remote from, and better understood by, the citizens they represent. To this end we should aim to develop the forms of community justice, both within and outside the courts, as described by David Faulkner in his *Introduction*. This involves support for the idea of greater community involvement, a greater sense of fairness being delivered and less concern about becoming involved with other parts of the system through fear of being compromised. This would help justify what Lord Chancellor Hailsham told magistrates in 1981 when he referred to their influence out of court, as well as on the bench, and described them as 'one of the characteristic institutions holding our society together'.

Endnotes

1. 34 Edw. 3, c.1.
2. Sir Edward Coke (1797 edn.), *Fourth Institute,* London: E & R Brooke, p.170.
3. W R Cornish and G de N Clark (1989), *Law and Society in England: 1750-1950,* London: Sweet & Maxwell, p.20.
4. *R v. Barron* (1820) All ER (1814-23), p.775.
5. 18 & 19 Vict., c. 126.
6. Auld, Sir Robin (2001), *Review of the Criminal Courts of England and Wales.* London: The Stationery Office.
7 Sir Thomas Skyrme (1991), *The History of the Justices of the Peace,* Chichester: Barry Rose Publishers, Vol. ii, p.421.

12

EXTENDING THE OFFICE OF MAGISTRATE IN ENGLAND AND WALES

Rod Morgan is Professor Emeritus of Criminal Justice at the University of Bristol and Visiting Professor at the Universities Police Science Institute at Cardiff University. He served as an active magistrate in Bath from 1975-1995 and was HM Chief Inspector of Probation for England and Wales (2001-4) and Chairman of the Youth Justice Board for England and Wales (2004-7). He is the author of many articles and books on aspects of criminal justice ranging across policing, youth justice, sentencing and prisoners rights. He is also a co-editor of the leading British text on criminology, *The Oxford Handbook of Criminology* (2012, Oxford: Oxford University Press), now in its fifth edition.

EXTENDING THE OFFICE OF MAGISTRATE IN ENGLAND AND WALES

Rod Morgan

It remains to be seen whether the Prime Minister and the Conservative Party persist with their talk of the Big Society, their 2010 election slogan that singularly failed to capture the public imagination and has since earned a good deal of derision and scepticism despite several re-launches (for a review see Morgan, 2012). But whichever interpretation of the Big Society one chooses to highlight, the lay magistracy must be accounted its archetypal embodiment.

Magistrates are unpaid *volunteers*, albeit they may claim modest loss of earnings. They dispense *local* justice, even if the court closure programme pursued by successive governments means that justice is now far less local than used to be the case. In terms of gender and race magistrates are considerably more *representative* of the public at large than any other practitioner group working within the criminal justice system. And, if the cost implications of differential sentencing practice are taken into account, magistrates are also *cost effective*: their infrastructural support costs may mean they are no cheaper than district judges to employ (Ipsos MORI, 2011), but when dealing with like-for-like cases they are significantly more parsimonious than their professional counterparts both with regard to use of custodial remands and sentences (Morgan and Russell, 2000). These considerations—a mixed economy in public services provision, localisation, enhanced democratisation and reduced costs — are fundamental to the Big Society vision. In which case, the future of the magistracy ought to be secure.

Yet there are question marks about the future. The lay magistracy may have comprised the core of the Anglo-Welsh justice system since the middle of the fourteenth century (Skyrme, 1994). The model may, during the period of Empire, have been bequeathed to numerous overseas territories. But, over time, virtually all those territories have, with independence and modernisation, largely abandoned the lay magistracy in favour of a full-time, paid, professional judiciary. The office is not even thriving within these islands. The Irish Republic abolished it in 1924. Lay magistrates in Scotland enjoy a very minor, residual role. And in Northern Ireland efforts have recently had to be made to revive the institution better to engage a more peaceful community in the dispensation of justice. England and Wales, uniquely, retains a system whereby lay magistrates hear the overwhelming majority of less serious criminal cases brought before the courts. Within the continental, Roman law tradition lay persons similar to magistrates are more akin to permanent juror panels sitting alongside professional judges hearing serious cases in the higher courts.

Nor is there confidence within the ranks. There has been a good deal of muted grumbling in magistrates' court retiring rooms over several decades. I have observed it both as an insider (I was appointed a JP in 1974) and as an outsider (in 1995 I resigned for want of time to undertake the required number of sittings, and was later debarred because I held posts, with the probation inspectorate and the Youth Justice Board, which were incompatible with the office). Bench amalgamations and court closures have always given rise to aggravation, including a few resignations. And recently there have been two additional gripes. First, the gradual increase in the number of district judges and the accusation that, like asset strippers, they get the more 'interesting' (politically sensitive) cases, and not necessarily those requiring prolonged sittings or more difficult points of law: the riot-related cases following the events of August 2011 being a case in point. Secondly, the granting to the police and Crown Prosecution Service (CPS) by the New Labour Government powers to impose summary out-of-court sanctions in many cases that would formerly have come to court. Many magistrates feel their jurisdiction is being squeezed from above and below, to such an extent that they are sceptical about ministerial blandishments that the Anglo-Welsh magistracy is the 'epitome of the *Big Society* in action' (Herbert, 2011).

Let us briefly examine this 'squeeze' before considering how the role of the magistracy might be extended.

There are currently some 140 district judges (and about the same number of part-time deputy district judges) relative to about 26,000 magistrates. A decade ago there were only 104 district judges relative to 30,400 magistrates (Auld, 2001: pp. 72-3). District judges have incontestably been appointed to displace magistrates. Nonetheless, magistrates still deal with about 90 per cent of the work in the summary courts and magistrates today have to deal with considerably less of the brain-numbing, minor business (for example, myriads of minor traffic offences invariably dealt with in a defendants' absence, largely by rote) that they were required to hear 20 or 30 years ago. It cannot seriously be contended that magistrates' court lists are intrinsically less interesting or intellectually demanding than previously: on the contrary, they have if anything been enriched, not impoverished. The asset-stripping consequences of having more district judges has by comparison been marginal.

The enrichment has resulted from the gradual extension of police and CPS powers administratively to impose penalties, initially for traffic offences (static, construction and moving) and then public order and other volume crimes. In my experience most magistrates have been grateful to be relieved of this mostly tedious business. That view has recently changed, however.

All jurisdictions provide their police and prosecutorial agencies with administrative powers to impose out-of-court summary penalties and the case for extending this trend was eloquently set out in 2006 by Lord Falconer, then Lord Chancellor. Public confidence in the criminal justice system had fallen. Many repeat minor offenders were not being brought to book. Criminal justice proceedings were 'often lengthy and arcane'. The solution, Lord Falconer contended, was 'to connect the instance of crime much more quickly and directly with the consequences of crime' (2006: 9). Granting the police and CPS powers to penalise more minor, admitted matters—defendants were guaranteed the right to have cases they did not admit brought to court—would enable the courts to devote more attention to more serious business. Better justice and increased public confidence would be the result, not least because the public would see offences undermining their quality of life being dealt with more speedily and effectively.

That was the plausible theory. But the question begged by Lord Falconer was whether the new out-of-court powers (warnings for possession of cannabis, penalty notices for disorder, conditional cautions and restorative disposals) would be used proportionately, equitably and accountably. From time to time various commentators, including representatives of the magistracy, have suggested that none of these conditions was satisfactorily being met and some supporting evidence for that contention was furnished in 2011 in a joint inspectorate report (HMCPS/IHMIC, 2011).

There are major differences not explained by differential crime patterns in the degree to which the new powers are being used in different police force areas and the inspectorates found that one third of the various out-of-court disposal cases scrutinised (admittedly a small sample) had been imposed inappropriately, that is, contrary to the rules and guidance. A minister of state has since divulged that Home Office statistics for 2011 indicate that 4.5 per cent of all offenders cautioned had previously received 15 or more cautions (Herbert, 2011). Further, the rationale for using the out-of-court disposals was rarely recorded (even though police policies require it) and oversight of decision-making by 'evidence review officers' did not extend to penalties decided on the street (HMIC/CPSI 2011: 23-24). All of which means that because some out-of-court penalties are being used inappropriately (for cases or offenders who should be brought before the court) the important principle of *proportionality of imposition* is being breached and there is a distinct absence of accountability. This is not a situation likely to inspire public let alone judicial confidence.

The Lord Chief Justice (2011) expressed concern that we are developing an incoherent threefold system of summary justice—that dealt with in the magistrates' courts, that dealt with out of court by the police, and now the possible development of neighbourhood resolution panels across the country (Ministry of Justice, 2011). He proposes that the police be required to account, by means of a periodic published statistical statement, how their out-of-court powers are being used locally. But it seems to me that there is a more substantial way of building confidence and accountability about the sensible use of administrative penalties, developing community-based restorative justice mechanisms and guarding the delicate boundary with the jurisdiction of the summary courts. That would be by making in each commission area a panel of lay magistrates responsible for *overseeing* the use of out-of-court penalties and NRPs, not just receiving statistical accounts regarding them.

No statistical report of the sort proposed by the Lord Chief Justice would assure that the police guidelines had been followed and the rationale for using out-of-court penalties had been recorded. Such an arrangement would not in any way subvert the independence of the police and their proper use of discretion, but it would make for greater transparency and accountability and it would sit comfortably alongside the cuts to police budgets which are in the pipeline and the introduction of directly elected police and crime commissioners. We will all need to be assured locally that justice is being done.

Whether the role of lay magistrates should be enhanced in another direction, namely by their acting as professional jurors sitting alongside judges in selected cases in the Crown Court, is also an interesting proposition worthy of consideration. But I will leave that question to be examined by Louis Blom-Cooper in *Chapter 2*.

References

Auld, Sir Robin (2001), *Review of the Criminal Courts of England and Wales,* London: The Stationery Office.

Falconer, Lord (2006), *Doing Law Differently*, London: Department of Constitutional Affairs.

Herbert N (2011), 'Reclaiming Summary Justice', Speech to the National Council of the Magistrates' Association, 8th December.

Judge, Lord Justice (2011), 'Summary Justice in and out of Court', *The Police Foundation John Harris Memorial Lecture,* London: Police Foundation.

Ipsos MORI (2011), *The Strengths and Skills of the Judiciary in the Magistrates' Courts*, London: Ministry of Justice.

Ministry of Justice (2011), *Testing Neighbourhood Resolution Panels: A Specification to Inform Expressions of Interest*, London: Ministry of Justice.

Morgan R (2012), 'Crime and Justice in the "Big Society"', *Criminology and Criminal Justice.*

Morgan R and Russell N (2000), *The Judiciary in the Magistrates Courts*, London: Lord Chancellor's Department/Home Office.

Skyrme T (1994), *History of the Justices of the Peace*, Chichester: Barry Rose Publications.

13

ALTERNATIVE FUTURES FOR THE MAGISTRACY?

Nicola Padfield is a Senior Lecturer at the Law Faculty, University of Cambridge. A barrister by training, she has published widely on criminal law, sentencing and criminal justice. Her books include *The Criminal Justice Process: Text and Materials* (4th edn., 2008); *Criminal Law* (8th edn., 2012); *Beyond the Tariff: Human Rights and the Release of Life Sentence Prisoners* (2002); *Who to Release? Parole, Fairness and Criminal Justice* (as editor, 2007); and *Release from Prison – European Policy and Practice* (co-editor with Dünkel and van Zyl Smit, 2011). She has edited other works and is the editor of *Archbold Review*. She sits as a Recorder (part-time judge) in the Crown Court and is a Bencher of the Middle Temple.

ALTERNATIVE FUTURES FOR THE MAGISTRACY?

Nicola Padfield

Introduction

It would be easy to construct an account of the slow demise of the lay magistracy in the late twentieth and early twenty-first century: most obviously in decades of court closures, but also in terms of numbers (of magistrates, of trials, and so on) and in terms of role (abolition of boards of visitors, police authorities, and so on). The opportunity to paint an alternative picture is welcome: this brief chapter argues that there is enormous scope for an increasing role for the lay judiciary today, by painting a picture of a vibrant magistracy offering swift open justice in court, and striving to ensure 'justice' across the wider criminal justice system. The starting point is the acknowledgement of the importance of an independent judiciary and the constitutional doctrine of the separation of powers: judges (and magistrates) are there to check that the Rule of Law, and legal rights, are upheld, to be vigilant that discretionary powers are not abused. To what extent this duty should be carried out by lay magistrates and not legally qualified professionals is a moot point. There are strong arguments for 'community justice', or local justice, and there is no obvious reason why an important role should not be played by lay magistrates, supported by, and working with, legal advisers and the professional judiciary.

Diversion from Court

The huge growth in out of court disposals has been noted elsewhere (see Padfield, Morgan, Maguire, 2012). Despite widespread recognition that this can lead to inconsistent and unfair decision-making, there is no evidence that the pressure to divert cases from court will reduce. There may have been a brief downturn in 2009-2010 as a result of a sudden political concern about the number of serious cases which were not prosecuted, but it would appear that financial cuts are now leading both the police and Crown Prosecution Service to look again for what they perceive as cheaper alternatives to prosecution.

It is of course impossible even to guess how many offenders are simply 'ticked off' by the police, or indeed their friends, families or employers. Even those who are detected and reported to the police are subject to a huge variety of alternative out-of-court disposals. In 2009, an astonishing 38 per cent of the 1.29 million offences 'solved' by police were dealt with outside of the court system. The joint report of HM Inspectorate of Constabulary/H.M. Inspectorate of the CPS (2011) usefully highlighted variations in use, ranging in different police force areas from 26 per cent to 49 per cent of all offences 'brought to justice'. In youth justice, the picture is even more confusing. New Labour abolished cautions for children in the Crime and Disorder Act 1998, replacing them with reprimands and warnings. But this system is being discarded in the Legal Aid, Sentencing and Punishment of Offenders Bill (going through Parliament at the time of writing).

It may well therefore be time for a serious review of these processes. Morgan (2008) argued that

> extensive net-widening has occurred over the past five or six years in the sense that many more children, young people and adults have been drawn into the criminal justice system, mostly through the use of pre-court sanctions.

This net-widening needs to be examined, quite as much as the questions of consistency and accountability. Lord Judge voiced the concerns of many when he asked in a speech in July 2011 whether the 'convenience' of avoiding the court process may lead an offender to admit to something for which he or she would have a defence. There could be, he suggested, an important role for magistrates in supervising out-of-court decision-making (Judge, 2011).

Trial Justice

Why are magistrates' courts being closed? As an economy, of course. Yet there are alternative messages even here. We hear of the advantages of 'problem-solving courts': dedicated drugs courts, mental health courts, and specialist domestic violence courts. The magistrates' court could and should be a classic problem-solving court. Another buzz concept is the neighbourhood justice panel: this could be a good definition of a magistrates' court. Similarly, we hear much about 'restorative justice'. A magistrates' court can facilitate this: of course there is a role for formal restorative justice conferencing, allowing victims of crime who wish to do so to meet their offender face-to-face, and to encourage offenders to repair the harm they caused. But it would be unduly negative (even dangerous?) to think that a magistrates' court itself cannot be restorative.

There are many reasons why the censure involved in sentencing should be done in public. Decisions on whether or not to convict someone of a crime, and decisions on the appropriate sentence, should be pronounced publicly, and be clearly explained. It is not for the police to impose significant 'sentences' behind closed doors. Tyler's work on procedural justice has been important in the academic world (see in particular Tyler, 2001). He suggests that people evaluate the police and the courts in terms of the fairness of the treatment that they (and others) receive from those authorities. Thus, if people

> feel that legal authorities are polite and respectful, sincere and benevolent, and do not harass or stigmatise community residents, they are more supportive of law and legal authorities (at p.234).

The courts play a vital role in helping to gain and retain the trust and confidence of people in the criminal justice system (Tyler, 2010).

The role of the magistrates' court was weakened by the creation of referral orders: young offenders being routinely referred to, or diverted to, the youth offending team (YOT) and youth offending panel (YOP). Why was this deemed to be necessary? Perhaps it was not so much a question of cost, but a feeling that magistrates' courts were less 'effective' than a YOT. Perhaps too it was because magistrates were perceived to be 'out of touch'? If this was the case, the solution could have been to improve the method of selection and appointment of magistrates. The real advantage of the YOT has been the multi agency work achieved with young offenders. But this comes at a price: multi-agency decision-making is rarely open and transparent. In fact, 'joining up' criminal justice agencies has become something of a panacea for the ills of the 'system'. For example, as well as youth offending teams, we have multi-agency public protection arrangements (MAPPAs). Whilst it is of course important that different agencies should work together to 'manage' offenders in the community, the need for transparency and accountability is ever more important. Could there be a role for magistrates here, overseeing the enormous powers exercised by these multi-agency bodies, out of sight even of the offender, let alone the public?

Post-trial Sentence Management

The Justice Committee of the House of Commons' report *Towards Effective Sentencing* (2008) adopted the term 'backdoor sentencing'. It is a useful term, since it encourages us to recognise that what judges and magistrates do when they sentence someone, is simply opening the 'front door' into the penal system. Currently, judges often have little feedback or involvement in the implementation or monitoring of sentences. Yet surely judicial review or supervision of the way sentences are carried out is essential. I argued in a series of short articles published in 2011, for serious consideration by English policy-makers of the French system of *aménagement des peines*: could we not adopt a system of *juges d'application des peines* into the English criminal justice system? (see Padfield, 2011) The French experience seems to suggest that active judicial involvement in sentence implementation impacts on offender compliance. Is a more judicialised system more expensive, or ultimately cheaper, than one which is less regulated?

The power (created in section 178 Criminal Justice Act 2003), allowing the Secretary of State to give criminal courts the power or duty to review community orders, has not been applied widely. Perhaps this is a question of cost. But a time of austerity may encourage original thinking. For example, Maruna and LeBel (2003) encourage us to think imaginatively about 'strengths-based re-entry courts'. Could magistrates develop a role for dispensing 'reintegration', through which a stigmatised person has the opportunity to 'make good'? Courts, of course, normally focus on punishing failures and not on rewarding positive achievements. Maruna (2011) suggests 'rituals of reintegration' powerful enough to counteract the 'status degradation ceremonies' of current criminal justice.

The huge increase in numbers of prisoners recalled to prison during the community part of their sentence is well known and deeply problematic (see Padfield, 2012). Currently, offenders are recalled to prison, in effect by the probation service (if this is an apt name for it today) and formally by the Minister of Justice via the National Offender Management Service (NOMS). Prisoners' files are reviewed by the Parole Board but the system is deeply inefficient, and widely perceived as unfair and one-sided. A court should review decisions to recall an offender to prison, and indeed should seek to help speed their progress towards re-release

A Wider Role

This leads to a discussion of the potential of the magistracy in a much wider role. The politically sensitive subject of police accountability is beyond the scope of this chapter. But it is worth noting that the number of magistrates on police authorities has been in decline for many decades, and now of course police authorities are being abolished. Whilst many commentators (including this one) regret their demise, we should remember that the police authority has not been the only mechanism by which chief constables are held to account. Interestingly, independent custody visitors, whose important role is to monitor activities within police stations, are currently specifically required not to be magistrates. This might be a good time to revisit whether police stations and policing more generally is adequately subject to judicial oversight.

Magistrates have had a strong historic role in overseeing prisons. In the sixteenth century, Visiting committees of justices were established for local prisons, and the visiting committees created by the Prison Act 1877 were made up entirely of magistrates. The boards of visitors which existed for a hundred years from 1898 until 1998 consisted of both JPs and non-JPs. Today's independent monitoring boards (IMBs) may include lay magistrates. 'Monitoring' was held to be incompatible with their judicial role in 'sentencing' offenders for breach of disciplinary offences. Now district judges are responsible for hearing serious cases of prison indiscipline (adjudications), and IMBs focus on monitoring the day-to-day life in the prison seeking to ensure that proper standards of care and decency are maintained. Could or should lay magistrates sit with district judges on adjudications? Why are lay magistrates no longer required to monitor their local prisons? The House of Commons' Justice Committee recently concluded (at paras 110-111):

> There needs to be a better, more seamless, approach to managing offenders. Prisoners are shunted between one establishment and another, in an attempt to avoid overcrowding, and the need to ensure continuity of their sentence plan is not a priority. This is unacceptable. The Ministry of Justice and NOMS need to devise and implement a strategy to ensure that the end-to-end management of offenders is a reality and not just an unachieved aspiration.

More judicial oversight, an improved system of checks and balances, might be valuable.

Every prison used to have a local review committee of the Parole Board. Their historic role is worth reconsidering: in the early days of parole (the late-1960s, early-1970s), as the Home Office realised how cautious the Parole Board had already become, they decided to release many prisoners automatically on the recommendation of the local review committee (Morgan, 1983). Sadly these committees were abolished in 1991, and the Parole Board has become increasingly cautious and under-resourced. Is it time to re-consider local review committees of the Parole Board—might these be magistrates' courts?

Conclusion

The present Government (like its predecessor) pays lip-service to the need to reform and to 're-energise' the criminal justice system, to 'reconnect with local communities'. Yet at the same time criminal justice appears to be becoming ever more fragmented (and privatised); the police role in the management of offenders is increasing, and the traditional distinctions between the roles of the probation service and of police officers are becoming blurred. The need for greater public accountability and for 'justice' is obvious. Justice requires open and transparent processes. The magistracy could have a greater role, and not just in deciding upon individual guilt in individual cases. The Magistrates Association is to be congratulated on encouraging a debate on the appropriate role for a lay magistracy in the twenty-first century.

References

House of Commons Justice Committee (2008), *Towards Effective Sentencing* (HC 184), London: Stationery Office.

House of Commons Justice Committee (2011), *The Role of the Probation Service* (HC 519-1), London: Stationery Office.

Lord Judge (2011), 'Summary Justice In and Out of Court', The Police Foundation's John Harris Memorial Lecture, www.judiciary.gov.uk/media/speeches/2011/lcj-speech-john harris-memorial-lecture-07072011

HM Inspectorate of Constabulary/HM Inspectorate of the CPS (2011), *Exercising Discretion: The Gateway to Justice*.

Maruna, S and LeBel T (2003), 'Welcome Home? Examining the "Re-entry Court" Concept from a Strengths-based Perspective', 4 *Western Criminology Review*, 91.

Maruna, S (2011), 'Re-entry as a Rite of Passage', *Punishment & Society*, 3.

Morgan, N (1983), 'The Shaping of Parole in England and Wales', Crim LR, 137.

Morgan, R (2008), *Summary Justice: Fast—But Fair?*

Padfield, N (2011), 'An Entente Cordiale in Sentencing?', 175 *Criminal Law and Justice Weekly*, 239, 256, 271 and 290.

Padfield, N (2012), 'Recalling Conditionally Released Prisoners in England and Wales' (2012), 4 *European Journal of Probation*, 34.

Padfield, N, Morgan, R and Maguire, M (2012), 'Out of Court, Out of Sight? Criminal Sanctions and Non-judicial Decision-making' in Maguire, Morgan, and

Reiner (eds.), *The Oxford Handbook of Criminology* (5th edn.), Oxford: Oxford University Press.

Tyler, T R (2001), 'Public Trust and Confidence in Legal Authorities: What Do Majority and Minority Group Members Want from the Law and Legal Institutions?', 19 *Behav. Sci. Law,* 215.

Tyler, T R (2010), 'Legitimacy in Corrections: Policy Implications', 9 *Criminology and Public Policy,* 127.

14

CHALLENGES FOR THE FAMILY JUSTICE SYSTEM

Malcolm Richardson has been a magistrate since 1979 and is currently deputy chairman of the Magistrates' Association where he leads on family justice issues (though he writes here in a personal capacity and the views expressed should not be taken as those of anyone other than him). He has been a bench chairman and chairman of the Avon and Somerset Justices' Issues Group. He was a founder member of the Family Justice Council and has been a member of a number of other judicial and inter-disciplinary bodies advising on policy and practice development in the family courts.

Following a corporate career with IBM, in 1994 he established a management consultancy practice which continues to provide his fee-earning focus (whilst enabling him to acquire knowledge of other jurisdictions' philosophy and approach to family justice during his overseas assignments).

He is a passionate advocate for the involvement of magistrates in family justice, firmly believing that the community-grounded, common sense life experiences of magistrates equip them with the pragmatism to deal with this most challenging of jurisdictions.

CHALLENGES FOR THE FAMILY JUSTICE SYSTEM

Malcolm Richardson

Fairly recently one could write about the family justice system and the place of magistrates within it confident that the environment would not change much. With the arrival of the Family Justice Review (FJR),[1] the Government's response[2] and the (by judicial standards) breakneck speed of implementation of many key recommendations, I cannot be certain that this chapter won't be out of date before I have finished drafting it — let alone by the time the publication date arrives.

However, in a book with an agenda such as this one, the inclusion of the work of magistrates in the family courts is highly appropriate, indeed vital. From a purely workload perspective it is the one jurisdiction involving magistrates where there is, sadly for the subject families, an increase in caseload.

The powers and responsibilities of magistrates authorised to sit in the family proceedings court (FPC) stem mostly from the Children Act 1989 and the Adoption and Children Act 2002. That magistrates' powers and involvement have stood the test of time is evidenced by the endorsement of that role (in the main) by the Norgrove Report (as the FJR is also known) — even if, anecdotally at least, one senior family judge reportedly complained that his postman (a family magistrate) had more powers than he had.

Significant changes are afoot, however. Whether they are to be welcomed by magistrates depends on how forward-looking and optimistic they are. The President of the Family Division, Sir Nicholas Wall, took a bold pre-emptive move in the wake of the FJR final report in appointing a senior Judge in Charge of the Modernisation of Family Justice (fortunately a time-limited appointment or that title would definitely have to go!). In selecting Sir Ernest Ryder to fill the post, the magistracy could not have hoped for a better supporter. Having worked first with him some eight years ago on the first Protocol for Judicial Case Management in Public Law Children Act Cases I know how empathic he is to and understanding of the unique nature, skills and value that magistrates bring to the judicial process.

The optimistic group of family magistrates will see the rejection by Nor-grove of an entirely professional family judiciary; the creation of a single, unified Family Court and their inclusion in it; greater inclusion in the family judicial community under the leadership of their designated family judge; creation of formal liaison and advice for a stronger voice in discussions with Her Majesty's Courts and Tribunal Service (HMCTS); enhanced protection for their judicial independence; the opportunity for more focussed advocacy for family justice training within a shrinking budget, etc. as clear evidence of an expanded future.

Nay-sayers will comment on the move of the single point of entry for public law cases from the FPC; the introduction of a gatekeeping allocation function without magistrates; the creation of a family justice governance infrastructure with no magistrate representation; fears of a reduction in hearing centres and/or the combining of panels; the moving of private law cases into alternative dispute resolution; the family ticketing of a whole raft of new district judges (magistrates' courts) without any apparent justification or plan; and ignorance or outdated prejudice on behalf of the full-time judiciary of the skills, competence and experience of family magistrates.

So what is my, entirely personal, view of the landscape and outlook?

Family magistrates have a once in a generation (where have I heard that phrase before) opportunity to help to shape part of the justice system and their place within it—but they won't do it without showing great(er) flexibility in the what, how and where of their involvement. Failure to grasp this opportunity will result in a slow (or in some areas fast) death except for some private law work at the edges. Those courts where benign neglect or wilful disregard by justices' clerks and their staffs of family justice, in cahoots with a full-time judiciary that doesn't understand or want to understand what magistrates can contribute, has resulted in negligible workload, and will not turn it round without magistrates taking the lead.

For the first time reliable data will start to appear consistently which will demonstrate those areas where FPCs do little work. They must grasp the evidence and challenge the outdated assumptions of their capacity and capability. They must recognise that, in a world where cases appear in court dramatically less often than now, and stay in the system a much shorter time, local access to a courtroom for families will be less important than now, and the advantages of a multi-courtroom hearing centre with a small cadre of experienced magistrates and full-time judiciary who can, in partnership confidently deal with cases expeditiously is, in most cases, the 'direction of travel'.

I understand the Cumbria or Cornwall question of provision in profoundly rural areas and it must be addressed—but that should not be used as an excuse in other places where maintenance of a host of small panels results in inefficient listing, uneconomic courthouse utilisation, half-day sittings, the impossibility of meaningful judicial continuity and an inadequate service to the most vulnerable families in society at their time of greatest need.

The call for judicial continuity will create different pressures on magistrates and the 'system' must recognise that this aim, running counter to the diversity agenda, will result in a less representative family magistracy than now. It may also cause even greater strain to the HMCTS mantra of efficiency and economy first and foremost (whatever happened to paramountcy of principle in children cases?). Of course, the meaning of 'judicial continuity' is still awaiting a convincing and common definition. It is evident through research that the Magistrates' Association has conducted that there is a clear distinction in the minds of most magistrates between judicial continuity and case management continuity which, in FPCs, falls to the legal adviser community. In my view, this latter is even more vital than the former — a responsibility that HMCTS seems not to have fully grasped yet (not least because it doesn't fit into a nicely defined box with a specific number of minutes attached to a specific task — professional discretion doesn't seem to be a concept that is well understood in the world of activity-based costing!).

If judicial continuity means the return of the entire bench for each hearing of a case then we may be aiming unachievably high. If it means at least one of the magistrates returning then that is more pragmatic, but we must grasp the challenge of understanding how we can ensure that the decision-making of the bench of three magistrates remains just that — of three equals — and does not become unbalanced in favour of the views or prior knowledge of the returning member(s) of an earlier tribunal. The last President of the Family Division, Sir Mark Potter, seemed to suggest that his interpretation of judicial continuity was through the chair alone. In accepting that definition then by implication he accepted such balance was achievable through training and common sense — two aspects of the magistrate's life and behaviour that are often ignored or neglected even though they are core to their appointment and ongoing authorisation to sit (and which other members of the judiciary can point to regular appraisal in justification of their authority to continue to adjudicate?).

Ofsted has recently observed that the bulk of the delays in adoption cases (and by implication care cases) arises through an excessive concern to allow assessments of parents and the extended family in order to try to keep children with their birth families.[3] Most magistrates would agree with that — but would Ofsted really advocate the opposite? There has rightly been much focus on reducing the involvement by and delay caused through the use of expert assessments particularly in public law cases. All the family magistrates I know could quote multiple cases where they were confident that such assessments would not significantly impact on their eventual decision-making (and would only serve to raise the hopes of desperate parents falsely) but did not feel they would get (or had got) support from the higher courts, and particularly the Court of Appeal in resisting the appointment of experts in such cases. This should not be interpreted as a justification for less involvement by the magistracy in family cases, but as a recognition that the whole judicial family needs to work together to solve the endemic problem of caution in the face of threats of human rights claims and an excessive focus on parents rather than children. It should always be remembered that both of the two key Acts mentioned above have 'children' in the title — neither has 'parent' or even 'family'.

There can be no doubt that the future (rapidly becoming the present) holds much change and many challenges for the family justice system. There is no reason why magistrates should not increase their involvement in it rather than the opposite. They have demonstrated their competence, their decisions are rarely appealed and even more than this they are rarely reversed. They are flexible, adaptable, available, reliable, resourceful — and free.

Endnotes

1. Norgrove D (2011), *Family Justice Review: Final Report,* London: Ministry of Justice and Department for Education, and Cardiff: Welsh Government.
2. (2012), *The Government's Response to the Family Justice Review: A System with Children and Families at its Heart,* Cm.8273. London: Ministry of Justice.
3. *Right on Time: Exploring Delays in Adoption* (2012), London: Ofsted. This report explores the effectiveness of arrangements to avoid delay in adoption outcomes for children in a sample of nine local authority areas and their partner agencies. The report draws on evidence from cases and from the views of adopters, children and young people and professionals, including local authority managers and social workers, and representatives from the Children and Family Court Advisory and Support Service (CAFCASS), the courts and the voluntary sector. See http://www.ofsted.gov.uk/resources/right-time-exploring-delays-adoption

15

THE HEART OF SUMMARY JUSTICE

Howard Riddle has been Senior District Judge (Chief Magistrate) since November 2010. He was appointed a Metropolitan Stipendiary Magistrate in 1995 and sat at Greenwich and Woolwich before moving to the City of Westminster Magistrates' Court in 2008. He was Deputy Chairman of the Sentencing Advisory Panel for four years, working closely with magistrates and others on the Magistrates' Courts Sentencing Guidelines now in force. He is an editor of *Wilkinson's Road Traffic Offences* (London: Sweet & Maxwell) and a (minor) contributor to the current edition of *Blackstone's Criminal Practice* (Oxford: Oxford University Press).

THE HEART OF SUMMARY JUSTICE

Howard Riddle

Will there be an unpaid magistracy, with non-lawyers at its heart, in the future? The answer is, without any doubt, yes. There are many reasons why this must be so. I will mention the two obvious constitutional reasons. England and Wales is unique in having a criminal justice system where no individual can be convicted, and remain convicted, of a criminal offence unless lay people (juries or magistrates) agree. If a district judge convicts at first instance, the defendant can exercise his or her right to a retrial by a judge and two magistrates in the Crown Court. The two magistrates can then outvote both the district judge and the judge at the Crown Court. Secondly, there is a real constitutional advantage to having lay people at the heart of the criminal justice system, bringing the community into the courtroom and the courtroom into the community.

I am told that some magistrates prefer not to be described as 'lay'. To me lay participation is a strength, not a weakness. The move towards professionalisation has been prompted, in part, by the increasing encroachment of complicated law and procedure into summary justice. Is not a better approach to try to remove these unnecessary complications? Magistrates are judges of fact and law. They do not need some of the processes that have been developed for jury trials. Take sections 76 and 78 Police and Criminal Evidence Act 1984, for example. This provides a process for a trial within a trial to exclude unfair evidence or unreliable confessions, so that juries do not hear tainted evidence. Magistrates do not need such a process. If we think the evidence is unfair or unreliable we simply attach no weight to it. I suggest that an appropriate goal for the next decade is to make summary justice accessible and intelligible to all. Allow magistrates to concentrate on fact-finding. Take away formulae that can obscure rather than clarify: *Turnbull* (on identification); *Lucas* (on lies); *Ghosh* (on dishonesty); good character and so on. Rely on magistrates to give clear and detailed reasons, particularly if convicting.

Training can then focus on fact-finding rather than law. In what circumstances might apparently convincing witnesses be mistaken about a positive identification? Why do innocent defendants sometimes lie to the police or even on oath? Can we tell from a person's demeanour whether that witness is lying? To what extent does the defendant's good or bad character assist our decision? What are the dangers of hearsay and what weight should we put on hearsay evidence? How can we tell whether an alleged victim of domestic violence lied to the police about the original complaint, or is now lying to the court when withdrawing that evidence? If a witness lies, does that mean we discount that person's evidence in its entirety? When does inconsistency undermine a case, and when is it normal and understandable? Fact-finding is often considered to be a matter of common sense, something that every citizen can do. Often it is. But is it always?

An incidental advantage of reducing the amount of complicated law in summary trials is that the premium on experience and expertise would also be reduced. There are, it seems to me, advantages in more members of the community serving as magistrates, but for shorter periods of time. Magistrates might be appointed initially for, say, a six-year term, and a proportion of those would be selected for a second term, primarily to serve as chairmen. Increasing the throughput would increase the constitutional significance of the magistracy, as mentioned above, and would probably reduce the average age of a magistrate. This in turn would mean that the many very valuable transferable skills learned by a magistrate could be used to serve the community in other ways after the six-year term is completed.

I would like to see magistrates recognised as specialists in fact-finding in summary cases. I know that many magistrates believe strongly that all magistrates should be able to undertake all work in a magistrates' court. That view may very well be correct, but it should at least be examined carefully. Would the fact-finding process sometimes be helped by having a magistrate on the bench with particular expertise in the area in dispute in a trial? For example, where there is expert evidence from a medical practitioner or a scientist. The magistrate would not of course substitute his or her views for that of the expert witness. It would be a question of ensuring that the bench as a whole properly understands and assesses the complicated expert evidence being brought before it. Similarly, in care cases in the family proceedings courts there is at least an argument that the quality of decision-making might be improved by having on the bench someone with experience in social work, of children's development, or teachers, or paediatric experts and so on, depending on the nature of the case.

Even if we manage to remove unnecessarily complicated law and practice from summary trials, there will inevitably remain some cases where the law is unusually difficult. I hope that most magistrates would accept that those cases are best reserved to the able and highly qualified lawyers who are now being appointed to the district bench.

I am satisfied that the best way forward for the magistracy is by close cooperation between judges and magistrates. I had the advantage of working with two former chairmen of the Magistrates' Association, Anne Fuller and Cindy Barnett, when the Sentencing Advisory Panel produced the draft Magistrates' Courts Sentencing Guidelines. They were later adopted by the Sentencing Guidelines Council. I believe those guidelines are now broadly welcomed as a very successful adjunct to the work of our courts. The group working on the draft guidelines met very regularly for well over a year. We didn't always agree. Sometimes discussions were heated. But those discussions were never sectarian. They always concentrated on the interests of justice. I am satisfied that the process of intense discussion between people from all backgrounds inside and outside the criminal justice system was a major component in the success of the guidelines. More recently I have worked closely with John

Thornhill, the preceding chair of the association, at whose request I have been happy to prepare this chapter. John is a master at expressing the views of the magistracy forcefully yet cooperatively. We worked together on Stop Delaying Justice!' At the time of writing it is too early to say whether all the objectives of that programme will be met. However it is certainly possible to say that most of those judges and magistrates who have worked closely together on developing and delivering the programme have found it a very valuable experience.

I will not say anything directly in this chapter about the areas where the jurisdiction of the magistrates' courts could be extended. Some of the other contributors to this book do so. What I will say is that the best way to extending our work is by ensuring that everybody understands that summary justice is as fair as any other form of justice.

Some of you will, like me, have heard with dismay the argument that a bishop accused of stealing two doughnuts should be entitled to trial by jury because of the importance of the case to his reputation. If the bishop is innocent and properly advised then he will without hesitation elect summary trial! In that way he can hope for his reputation to be restored within a matter of weeks, whereas trial by jury will inevitably take far longer to determine. Nowadays (and this was not the position until comparatively recently) he will see the evidence before the trial. The bench will give reasons for its decision. And in the very unlikely event of a miscarriage of justice there is an unrestricted right of appeal by way of rehearing to a Crown Court consisting of a judge and two magistrates. If however the bishop is guilty, then that might be a different story!

Summary justice is already a system of which we can be proud. We can improve it, particularly by removing unnecessary delay and unnecessary complications. We have demonstrated that we are competent to deal with all manner of cases, however complicated, lengthy or technical. Magistrates will remain at the heart of summary justice, as experts in fact-finding, giving a well-reasoned judgment, understandable by all and without jargon, and soon after the events.

Endnotes

1. See http://www.crimeline.info/stop-delaying-justice/

INDEX